Maven

A Developer's Notebook™

Other Java™ resources from O'Reilly

Related titles

Ant: The Definitive Guide

Apache: The Definitive Guide

Better, Faster, Lighter Java™

Beyond Java™

Building Better Software

Eclipse

Eclipse Cookbook™

Enterprise JavaBeans

Head First Java™

Head First EJB™

Head First Design Patterns

Hibernate: A Developer's Notebook

Jakarta Commons Cookbook™

Jakarta Struts Cookbook™

Java™ and XML

Java™ Enterprise in a Nutshell

Java™ in a Nutshell

JavaServer™ Faces

JBoss at Work: A Practical Guide

JBoss: A Developer's Notebook

JUnit Pocket Guide

JUnit: The Definitive Guide

Learning Java™

Programming Jakarta Struts

Spring: A Developer's Notebook

Unit Test Frameworks

Java Books Resource Center

java.oreilly.com is a complete catalog of O'Reilly's books on Java and related technologies, including sample chapters and code examples.

OnJava.com is a one-stop resource for enterprise Java developers, featuring news, code recipes, interviews, weblogs, and more.

Conferences

O'Reilly brings diverse innovators together to nurture the ideas that spark revolutionary industries. We specialize in documenting the latest tools and systems, translating the innovator's knowledge into useful skills for those in the trenches. Visit *conferences.oreilly.com* for our upcoming events.

Safari Bookshelf (*safari.oreilly.com*) is the premier online reference library for programmers and IT professionals. Conduct searches across more than 1,000 books. Subscribers can zero in on answers to time-critical questions in a matter of seconds. Read the books on your Bookshelf from cover to cover or simply flip to the page you need. Try it today with a free trial.

Maven
A Developer's Notebook™

Vincent Massol and Timothy O'Brien

O'REILLY®

Beijing · Cambridge · Farnham · Köln · Paris · Sebastopol · Taipei · Tokyo

Maven: A Developer's Notebook™
by Vincent Massol and Timothy O'Brien

Editor:	Mike Loukides
Production Editor:	Colleen Gorman
Cover Designer:	Emma Colby
Interior Designer:	David Futato

Printing History:

June 2005:	First Edition.

 RepKover™. This book uses RepKover™, a durable and flexible lay-flat binding.

ISBN: 0-596-00750-7

[M]

Contents

Foreword

Maven is an incredibly boring technology. That's right, I said boring. If you use Maven, your development infrastructure will be so coherent, predictable, and reproducible that you won't even think about it anymore. Your development infrastructure will just work. Period. No more excitement when you're getting down to the wire and your bonus is on the line; you won't have to worry about whether your build will suddenly screw up, forcing you to miss your launch date.

It's pretty amazing: Apple has built a business around things that just work. But software developers haven't held themselves to the same kinds of standards: they're perfectly willing to build brittle development environemnts filled with inconsistent ad-hoc hacks just waiting to trip them up. Imagine if your other tools were equally reliable: if, when you flipped a light switch, sparks suddenly started flying; if, when you flushed the toilet, it suddenly decided to flush up. But that's the sort of environment in which we software developers have lived for many years.

A successful technology takes away a burden, rather than imposing one. You don't have to worry about whether or not it's going to work; you don't have to jump through hoops trying to get it to work; it should rarely, if ever, be part of your thought processes. It should just work, in the background, shielding you from complexities and allowing you to think about the important problems. That's why I started the Maven project. You shouldn't have to know about the gory details of your build infrastructure; it should simply work. Because Maven is boring, your organization can focus on adding value to your core technologies instead of mucking about with development infrastructure.

Technologies are rarely fully transparent, and Maven is no exception. There is a learning curve, particularly if you're bring Maven's project management capabilities to an existing project. The Maven community is fortu-nate indeed to have Vincent Massol and Tim O'Brien, who have taken the time to bring the first Maven book to the community. Vincent has been a key member of the Maven community since the early days; he's done a lot of evangelism, written many plug-ins, and has contributed a lot of feed-back that was being incorporated into Maven 2. Tim hasn't been as visi-ble in the Maven community itself, but has been influential in getting Maven adopted by a number of other open source projects. Together, they have created a very practical and informative guide that will help you and your organization deploy Maven successfully.

Everyone needs some excitement. But you don't want your thrills to come from wondering whether your build process will break at a crucial moment. In the long run, there's nothing less exciting, and few things more painful, than a broken project environment. If you agree with me, Tim and Vincent are going to help you to make your life more exciting and interesting by making your build process as boring and reliable as it should be.

—Jason van Zyl
CTO, Mergere
Founder, Apache Maven Project
Los Angeles, April, 2005

The Developer's Notebook Series

So, you've managed to pick this book up. Cool. Really, I'm excited about that! Of course, you may be wondering why these books have the odd-looking, college notebook sort of cover. I mean, this is O'Reilly, right? Where are the animals? And, really, do you *need* another series? Couldn't this just be a cookbook? How about a nutshell, or one of those cool hacks books that seems to be everywhere? The short answer is that a developer's notebook is none of those things—in fact, it's such an important idea that we came up with an entirely new look and feel, complete with cover, fonts, and even some notes in the margin. This is all a result of trying to get something into your hands you can actually use.

It's my strong belief that while the nineties were characterized by everyone wanting to learn everything (Why not? We all had six-figure incomes from dot-com companies), the new millennium is about information pain. People don't have time (or the income) to read through 600 page books, often learning 200 things, of which only about 4 apply to their current job. It would be much nicer to just sit near one of the uber-coders and look over his shoulder, wouldn't it? To ask the guys that are neck-deep in this stuff why they chose a particular method, how they performed this one tricky task, or how they avoided that threading issue when working with piped streams. The thinking has always been that books can't serve that particular need—they can inform, and let you decide, but ultimately a coder's mind was something that couldn't really be captured on a piece of paper.

This series says that assumption is patently wrong—and we aim to prove it.

A Developer's Notebook is just what it claims to be: the often-frantic scribbling and notes that a true-blue alpha geek mentally makes when working with a new language, API, or project. It's the no-nonsense code that solves problems, stripped of page-filling commentary that often serves more as a paperweight than an epiphany. It's hackery, focused not on what is nifty or might be fun to do when you've got some free time (when's the last time that happened?), but on what you need to simply "make it work." This isn't a lecture, folks—it's a lab. If you want a lot of concept, architecture, and UML diagrams, I'll happily and proudly point you to our animal and nutshell books. If you want every answer to every problem under the sun, our omnibus cookbooks are killer. And if you are into arcane and often quirky uses of technology, hacks books simply rock. But if you're a coder, down to your core, and you just want to get on with it, then you want a Developer's Notebook. Coffee stains and all, this is from the mind of a developer to yours, barely even cleaned up enough for print. I hope you enjoy it...we sure had a good time writing them.

Notebooks Are...

Example-driven guides

As you'll see in the "Organization" section, developer's notebooks are built entirely around example code. You'll see code on nearly every page, and it's code that *does something*—not trivial "Hello World!" programs that aren't worth more than the paper they're printed on.

Aimed at developers

Ever read a book that seems to be aimed at pointy-haired bosses, filled with buzzwords, and feels more like a marketing manifesto than a programming text? We have too—and these books are the antithesis of that. In fact, a good notebook is incomprehensible to someone who can't program (don't say we didn't warn you!), and that's just the way it's supposed to be. But for developers...it's as good as it gets.

Actually enjoyable to work through

Do you really have time to sit around reading something that isn't any fun? If you do, then maybe you're into thousand-page language references—but if you're like the rest of us, notebooks are a much better fit. Practical code samples, terse dialogue centered around practical examples, and even some humor here and there—these are the ingredients of a good developer's notebook.

About doing, not talking about doing

If you want to read a book late at night without a computer nearby, these books might not be that useful. The intent is that you're coding as you go along, knee deep in bytecode. For that reason, notebooks talk code, code, code. Fire up your editor before digging in.

Notebooks Aren't...

Lectures

We don't let just anyone write a developer's notebook—you've got to be a bona fide programmer, and preferably one who stays up a little too late coding. While full-time writers, academics, and theorists are great in some areas, these books are about programming in the trenches, and are filled with instruction, not lecture.

Filled with conceptual drawings and class hierarchies

This isn't a nutshell (there, we said it). You won't find 100-page indices with every method listed, and you won't see full-page UML diagrams with methods, inheritance trees, and flow charts. What you will find is page after page of source code. Are you starting to sense a recurring theme?

Long on explanation, light on application

It seems that many programming books these days have three, four, or more chapters before you even see any working code. I'm not sure who has authors convinced that it's good to keep a reader waiting this long, but it's not anybody working on *this* series. We believe that if you're not coding within ten pages, something's wrong. These books are also chock-full of practical application, taking you from an example in a book to putting things to work on your job, as quickly as possible.

Organization

Developer's Notebooks try to communicate different information than most books, and as a result, are organized differently. They do indeed have chapters, but that's about as far as the similarity between a notebook and a traditional programming book goes. First, you'll find that all the headings in each chapter are organized around a specific task. You'll note that we said *task*, not *concept*. That's one of the important things to get about these books—they are first and foremost about doing something. Each of these headings represents a single *lab*. A lab is just what it sounds like—steps to accomplish a specific goal. In fact, that's the first heading you'll see under each lab: "How do I do that?" This is the central question of each lab, and you'll find lots of down-and-dirty code and detail in these sections. Many labs offer alternatives and address common questions about different approaches to similar problems. These are the "What about..." sections, which will help give each task some context within the programming big picture.

And one last thing—on many pages, you'll find notes scrawled in the margins of the page. These aren't for decoration; they contain tips, tricks, insights from the developers of a product, and sometimes even a little humor, just to keep you going. These notes represent part of the overall communication flow—getting you as close to reading the mind of the developer-author as we can. Hopefully they'll get you that much closer to feeling like you are indeed learning from a master.

And most of all, remember—these books are...

All Lab, No Lecture

—Brett McLaughlin, Series Creator

Preface

What is Maven? The Maven web site (*http://maven.apache.org*) states the following:

> Maven is a software project management and comprehension tool. Based on the concept of a Project Object Model (*POM*), Maven can manage a project's build, reporting, and documentation from a central piece of information.

While this captures the idea of Maven, it doesn't really explain what Maven is about. Here's another attempt: Maven provides a rich development infrastructure (compilation, testing, reporting, collaboration, and documentation) from a simple description of any Java project. It is an easy way to build a project without having to build a build system.

Maven started as an attempt to simplify and standardize the complex, Ant-based build process used for Jakarta Turbine. As the build system became more baroque and the Turbine project split into smaller, more focused components, a need emerged for a tool to describe each subproject and manage dependencies. The complexity of this multiproject Ant build created an ideal environment for a new project management system, and Maven 1 is the product of this natural evolution. Maven is frequently compared to the current build tool of choice—Apache Ant. And, while Maven is the clear successor to build systems built around Apache Ant, such a statement tends to cause some controversy... Maven 1 reuses a number of Ant tasks, and when you customize a Maven 1 build, you will end up using the tools that Ant provides. Maven is on a higher conceptual level than Ant; where Ant provides tools such as `mkdir` and `copy`, Maven is a build container which provides a common build process—a development infrastructure.

Maven captures best practices and codifies a common build process in a way that can be shared across all projects. When you "mavenize" a project, you create a project descriptor which describes the content and form of a project. This description is then used by common plug-ins which compile, test, package, and deploy project artifacts. In other words, you point Maven at your problem, and it takes care of the solution; you tell Maven where your source code resides, and it takes care of the compilation with little interference from you. You tell Maven to create a WAR file or create a JUnit report, and it retrieves the necessary libraries automatically. Maven is part automation, part build process, and part project description. If you are using Maven properly, you'll find yourself spending less time working on your project's build system and more time working on your project's code.

Just as Maven was inspired by the needs of the Jakarta Turbine project, Jakarta Ant was initially created as a part of the Jakarta Tomcat project. Ant spread like wildfire once people realized it had the potential to simplify project builds. Here's a quote from the Apache Ant FAQ (*http:// ant.apache.org/faq.html*) about the spread of Ant in 1999–2000:

> Soon thereafter, several open source Java projects realized that Ant could solve the problems they had with Makefiles. Starting with the projects hosted at Jakarta and the old Java Apache project, Ant spread like a virus and is now the build tool of choice for a lot of projects.

People used to use Makefiles for Java?! Yes, and it wasn't pretty.

When Ant was introduced, it revolutionized the community; Ant went from a novelty to an indispensable utility in the course of a year. Maven is experiencing a similar transition point as developers start to see how much easier it is to develop with a project management tool.

The Future: Maven 2

At the time of this writing, the initial technology preview for Maven 2 is available from the Maven web site (*http://maven.apache.org*). Although Maven 2 shares lots of concepts with Maven 1, it is a complete rewrite, and builds created for Maven 1 will not be compatible with Maven 2. Maven 1 plug-ins will not be directly compatible with Maven 2 plug-ins, and Jelly has been abandoned as a core scripting language. There will be migration paths, though. This book is peppered with references to Maven 2 and how Maven 2 differs from Maven 1. New features in Maven 2 include:

- Performance

  Fewer dependencies
    Maven's core drops the dependency on Jelly and Ant.

  Embeddable
    Maven 2 is designed to be embedded in other tools.

  Less Jelly, more Java
    Writing more logic in Java will mean faster execution.

- Lifecycle mechanism and definition

  Defined lifecycle

  Maven 2 defines a project's lifecycle, and plug-ins hook onto a particular part of that lifecycle. Instead of defining preGoals, postGoals, or prereqs, plug-ins tell Maven where they fit into the defined lifecycle.

  Multiproject aware

  Maven will work with multiple projects by default, and it will be easier to create multiproject builds.

- Dependency management

  Repository improvements

  Maven 2 will support a new, more-scaleable repository layout (explained in Chapter 1).

  Snapshots

  The mechanism for obtaining *SNAPSHOT* dependencies will be more configurable. You will be able to configure how often Maven checks for a new snapshot.

  Transitive dependencies

  Maven 2 will allow you to depend on a dependency's dependencies… confusing? If project A depends on artifact B, which in turn depends on artifact C, Maven 2's transitive dependency management will automatically retrieve and include artifact C in project A's dependencies.

- Customization and plug-ins

  No properties files or maven.xml files

  Behavior is now customized in the POM, which will be stored in *pom.xml*.

  No Jelly script

  Jelly script will no longer be the core scripting language for goals and plug-ins. For performance reasons, plug-in developers will be encouraged to write plug-ins in Java. Support for scripting languages such as Groovy and Marmalade will be available. A Jelly bridge will be available in Marmalade to easily port existing Maven 1 builds to Maven 2.

Many developers and businesses tend to wait anywhere from a few months to a few years to adopt a new project, and Maven 1 will remain in use for a long time as the feature set of Maven 2 is solidified and Maven 2 has time to prove itself. A final release of Maven 2 should be available in August or September of 2005, and plug-ins will be ported to

Maven 2 as developers move to the 2.0 release. Please note that the previous sentence was an estimate; providing a solid date for the release of a software project is an impossible feat, but based on progress at the time of this writing, Maven 2 is well within reach.

How This Book Is Organized

This book is a hybrid of styles. It is both a linear progression of ideas which will accelerate your introduction to Maven, and a collection of independent chapters and labs to be used as a reference. If you are already familiar with Maven, you may want to skim Chapters 1 and 2 before reading the rest of this book, as Chapters 1 and 2 introduce Maven 1 in the context of the upcoming Maven 2 release. If you are new to Maven, read the first chapter, before you move on to the more-advanced Maven topics in Chapters 3 through 6.

The content of this book is organized into chapters which consist of a series of labs or exercises. Within a chapter, each exercise builds upon the previous exercises. The book contains the following chapters:

Chapter 1, *Maven Jump-Start*
> Gets you up and running with Maven in less than an hour. If you are new to Maven, read this chapter first, as it lays the foundation for the following chapters.

Chapter 2, *Customizing Maven*
> While Maven provides default behavior sufficient for almost any project, there will be a situation that calls for customization of the build process. This chapter demonstrates the creation of custom goals, preGoals and postGoals, and the use of Jelly script and properties files to customize the behavior of Maven.

Chapter 3, *Multiproject Maven*
> This series of labs will teach you how to break a complex project into a series of smaller, related subprojects. Maven can be used to manage the dependencies between a set of projects, and you will see how Maven can be used to separate a web application into multiple projects.

Chapter 4, *Project Reporting and Publishing*
> Maven plug-ins provide a series of reports which provide a useful set of metrics for any project. This chapter demonstrates the use of reports to report on code quality, unit tests, code duplication, and project activity. This chapter also demonstrates how you can use Maven to publish and deploy project artifacts.

Chapter 5, *Team Collaboration with Maven*

Introduces a process for sharing a Maven installation and creating a custom remote repository for your team. The bulk of this chapter shows you how to use Maven to set up a continuous integration environment using CruiseControl.

Chapter 6, *Writing Maven Plug-ins*

Shows you how to build both simple and complex Maven plug-ins. A simple JAR execution plug-in is developed, and a plug-in involving Aspect-oriented programming is introduced.

Appendix, Maven Plug-ins

Lists all of the Maven plug-ins used in this book, and it provides instructions for installing plug-ins not bundled with Maven 1.0.2.

How This Book Was Written

This book is a result of collaboration between Vincent Massol and Tim O'Brien. Vincent drove the advanced Maven content, such as the chapters dealing with multiproject builds and custom plug-ins, and Tim wrote the introductory material found in Chapters 1 and 2.

Book content was developed using Microsoft Word files stored in a Subversion repository. A preliminary outline was developed using Atlassian's Confluence wiki, and simple task lists were maintained using Atlassian's JIRA issue tracker.

About This Book's Web Site

This book is supplemented by a web site—*http://www.mavenbook.org*—which contains updates and information about this book and about Maven. The web site will have additional sample applications and an aggregation of Maven-related blogs which you will find helpful as you follow this book and want to learn more about Maven.

You may check out errata, view related resources and online articles, and see the latest on this book, at *http://www.mavenbook.org* and *http://www.oreilly.com/catalog/mavenadn/*. Check these sites often; lots of new content may be available as time goes by and we update the examples.

About This Book's Examples

You can check out the sample Maven projects for this book from a Subversion repository maintained at *http://www.mavenbook.org/svn/mdn/code.*

To download Subversion and check out the code from the repository, follow these instructions from the *c:\dev\mavenbook* directory on Windows, or the *~/dev/mavenbook* directory on Unix:

1. Download Subversion from *http://subversion.tigris.org/project_packages.html.*

2. Install Subversion and add svn to your PATH.

3. Check out the code examples by executing the following command:

```
svn checkout http://www.mavenbook.org/svn/mdn/code mavenbook/code
```

Once you check out this project, you should have five subdirectories, each containing projects and subprojects relating to each chapter:

```
/mavenbook/code
  /genapp
  /plugins
  /qotd
  /reporting
  /weather
```

If you do not have access to Subversion or want to download an archive of the sample Maven projects from this book, visit the Maven Developer Notebook page at the O'Reilly web site at *http://www.oreilly.com/catalog/mavenadn/* or you can visit *http://www.mavenbook.org/download* to download an archive.

About the Authors

Vincent Massol has been an active participant in the Maven community as both a committer and a member of the Project Management Committee (PMC) since Maven's early days in 2002. Vincent has directly contributed to Maven 1's core as well as to various Maven plug-ins, including Cactus, JBoss, StatCvs, AspectJ, Changes, Clover, Eclipse, EAR, Dashboard, Multichanges, Aspectwerkz, Jetty, and Abbot. In addition to his work on Maven, he founded the Jakarta Cactus project—a simple testing framework for server-side Java code. Vincent lives and works in Paris, where he is the technical director of Pivolis, a company which specializes in collaborative offshore software development using Agile methodologies. This is Vincent's second book; he is a co-author of *JUnit in Action*, published by Manning in 2003 (ISBN 1-930-11099-5).

Tim O'Brien came to know Maven in his work with the Jakarta Commons community, where he formed part of the team that helped nudge projects toward Maven as a project management tool. Tim is an independent consultant living and working in Evanston, IL, just north of Chicago. This is

Tim's second book. He is the author of *Jakarta Commons Cookbook*, published by O'Reilly in 2004 (ISBN 0-596-00706-X).

Conventions Used in This Book

Italics are used for:

- Pathnames, filenames, program names, compilers, options, and commands
- New terms where they are defined
- Internet addresses, such as domain names and example URLs

`Constant width` is used for:

- Anything that appears literally in a JSP page or a Java program, including keywords, datatypes, constants, method names, variables, class names, and interface names
- Command lines and options that should be typed verbatim on the screen
- All JSP and Java code listings
- HTML documents, tags, and attributes
- XML element and attribute names
- Maven goals such as `java:compile`

`Constant width italics` are used for:

- General placeholders that indicate that an item is replaced by some actual value in your own program

`Constant width bold` is used for:

- Text that is typed on the command line
- Emphasis in source code

To indicate a continued command line, we used the convention appropriate to the operating system: \ for Unix, and ^ for a Windows DOS shell.

TIP

Designates a note, which is an important aside to the nearby text.

WARNING

Designates a warning relating to the nearby text.

Using Code Examples

This book is here to help you get your job done. In general, you may use the code in this book in your programs and documentation. You do not need to contact us for permission unless you're reproducing a significant portion of the code. For example, writing a program that uses several chunks of code from this book does not require permission. Selling or distributing a CD-ROM of examples from O'Reilly books *does* require permission. Answering a question by citing this book and quoting example code does not require permission. Incorporating a significant amount of example code from this book into your product's documentation *does* require permission.

We appreciate, but do not require, attribution. An attribution usually includes the title, author, publisher, and ISBN. For example: "*Maven: A Developer's Notebook*, by Vincent Massol and Tim O'Brien. Copyright 2005 O'Reilly Media, Inc., 0-596-00750-7."

If you feel your use of code examples falls outside fair use or the permission given above, feel free to contact us at *permissions@oreilly.com*.

How to Contact Us

Please address comments and questions concerning this book to the publisher:

O'Reilly Media, Inc.
1005 Gravenstein Highway North
Sebastopol, CA 95472
(800) 998-9938 (in the United States or Canada)
(707) 829-0515 (international or local)
(707) 829-0104 (fax)

We have a web page for this book, where we list errata, examples, and any additional information. You can access this page at:

http://www.oreilly.com/catalog/mavenadn/

To comment or ask technical questions about this book, send email to:

bookquestions@oreilly.com

For more information about our books, conferences, Resource Centers, and the O'Reilly Network, see our web site at:

http://www.oreilly.com

Safari® Enabled

 When you see a Safari® Enabled icon on the cover of your favorite technology book, it means the book is available online through the O'Reilly Network Safari Bookshelf.

Safari offers a solution that's better than e-books. It's a virtual library that lets you easily search thousands of top technology books, cut and paste code samples, download chapters, and find quick answers when you need the most accurate, current information. Try it for free at *http://safari.oreilly.com*.

Acknowledgments

Our reviewers were *essential* to the writing process. Special thanks to Dion Almaer, Felipe Leme, Henri Yandell, Carlos Sanchez, Arnaud Heritier, Guillaume Laforge, Brett Porter, Trygve Laugstol, Bob McWirther, David Blevins, Anton Mazkovoi, Emmanuel Venisse, and Jason van Zyl.

Thanks to our editor, Mike Loukides, for your wise guidance and advice. Thanks to our copy editor, Audrey Doyle, for putting up with our schedule and problems with the English language. Thanks to Colleen Gorman, and everyone involved in the production effort. Thanks also to Clay Andres of Studio B.

Credit must be given to Atlassian and Mike Cannon-Brookes for the collaborative software used to develop content for this book. This book was created using both Confluence and JIRA as essential communication tools. Confluence is a wiki and JIRA is an issue tracker; if you haven't used either, check out the Atlassian site at *http://www.atlassian.com*, and, after reading this book, you should take a look at the Maven JIRA plug-in. Thanks to the XWiki project, which is hosting the *mavenbook.org* wiki. If you're in need of a next-generation wiki, make sure to check XWiki at *http://www.xwiki.com*.

Thanks to the Subversion team (*http://subversion.tigris.org*) for developing the solid version control system in which this book was developed. Thanks to the Codehaus community (*http://www.codehaus.org*). And, thanks to the dedicated volunteers at the Apache Software Foundation (*http://www.apache.org*) for providing a structure that encourages the development of great software.

Acknowledgments from Vincent

If you're enjoying this book, you can thank Tim. He's made it enjoyable to read, transforming my technical prose into proper English. He also deserves credit for writing the first two chapters which are always treacherous to write, as they contain introductory material and it's hard to follow a linear progression and not jump ahead. In addition, Tim is also hosting the book's Subversion repository that we are using to serve the code to you. Thanks Tim!

I'd like to thank all the Maven developers who kindly agreed to take some of their Maven coding time to review the book. You can't imagine how priceless this is!

This book is the fruit of a long chain of events that can be traced back to the end of 1981, the year in which my parents had the insight to bring home one of the first IBM PCs. Since that time I've not stopped loving computers and programming them. I thank my parents for this, but even more for the caring and loving environment they provided during all those years.

Last, but not least, thanks to my wife, Marie-Albane, and my kids, Pierre-Olivier and Jean, who have allowed me, once again, to take some of their time and devote it to this book. A final acknowledgment goes to for my third and yet-to-be kid, still in the womb of his mother, who may even like Maven someday. Who knows?

Acknowledgments from Tim

Vincent Massol must get primary credit for leading this effort with excitement and energy. Truth be told, this is mostly Vincent's book, and he is the driving force behind much of the content. My main contributions were Chapters 1 and 2, and helping to review and format Vincent's chapters. Vincent has managed to pack Chapters 3, 4, 5, and 6 with challenging and engaging content I had thought impossible to introduce in such a format. Without Vincent, this book would have never happened, and he should get extra credit for putting up with my frequent disappearances. Vincent's contributions to open source development, unit testing, and agile development benefit the industry as a whole.

I'd like to thank the Institute for the International Education of Students, First Look, Lakunas, Saforian, and Grassroots Technologies. Thanks especially to Mike O'Brien, Rock Podrazik, Peter Costa, Kyle McCluskey, David McGarry, Andy Carlson, Paul Brown, Tim Beynart, Todd Rice, Stefan Winz, Pat Ryan, David Navin, Mark Snell, and Sam Luridas. Thanks to

Dr. Bryan Pfaffenberger and Dr. Stephen H. Jones. Also, thanks to the Chicago Java User Group (CJUG) for putting up with my Maven presentation, and thanks to Anil Saldhana, Bill Burke, and Kabir Khan of JBoss for helpful feedback.

Thanks to my supportive family in Chicago and on the East Coast. Last, but not least, thanks to my perfect wife, Susan O'Brien, and our yet-to-be-born child, who also may like Maven someday. Again, who knows?

CHAPTER 1

Maven Jump-Start

Let's start using Maven. By the end of this chapter you should be able to create a Maven project from scratch, use Maven to manage dependencies, and create a simple project web site with some interesting reports.

Installing Maven

Before you start in on this book, you'll need to install some prerequisites. While the examples in this book were written with Java 1.4.2, Maven is compatible with both Java 1.4.2 and Java 1.5.0. This book was written to the most recent version of Maven released at the time of this writing—Maven 1.0.2. In addition to the JDK and Maven 1.0.2, you will also need to be connected to the Internet, as Maven will download dependencies from a public web site as they are required. So, go ahead, install Maven.

TIP

Some of the plug-ins referenced in this Developer's Notebook are not bundled with Maven 1.0.2. Please refer to Chapter 6 and the comprehensive list of plug-ins in Appendix A for detailed instructions on installing the required Maven plug-ins.

How do I do that?

Download Maven from the Apache Software Foundation (ASF). Go to *http://maven.apache.org/* and select Downloading from the Getting Maven menu on the left navigation menu. This will take you to a page which will let you select a Windows Installer package, a *.zip* file, a tar'd *.bzip* file, or a tar'd *.gzip* file. Download the distribution appropriate for your platform.

On a Microsoft Windows platform, download the Windows Installer package (*maven-1.0.2.exe*) and follow the instructions during the automated installation. After Maven is installed using Windows Installer, you should have a user environment variable, MAVEN_HOME, pointing to the location of your Maven installation. You will then need to add %MAVEN_HOME%\bin to your PATH by selecting Control Panel→System→Advanced and clicking the Environment Variables button. Prepend %MAVEN_HOME%\bin to your PATH variable, and go to the command prompt by running *cmd.exe*. If Maven has been installed successfully, you should see the following output on the command line:

```
C:\dev\mavenbook\code>maven -v

 __  __
|  \/  |__ _Apache__ ___
| |\/| / _` \ V / -_) ' \   ~ intelligent projects ~
|_|  |_\__,_|\_/\_\___|_||_|  v. 1.0.2
```

If you prefer to install Maven in a directory other than *C:\Program Files\ Apache Software Foundation\Maven 1.0.2*, you may also download the Maven 1.0.2 *.zip* file and unpack Maven in any directory. Set MAVEN_HOME to point to the directory that holds the unpacked Maven distribution, and add MAVEN_HOME\bin to your PATH.

On a Unix platform, download the tar'd *.gzip* file (*maven-1.0.2.tar.gz*) and unpack it to the directory of your choice with tar xvzf maven-1.0.2. tar.gz. For this lab, we'll assume that you unpacked Maven to the */usr/ local/maven-1.0.2* directory. You will then need to set two environment variables, MAVEN_HOME and PATH. The following commands set these two variables to the appropriate values:

```
[tobrien@mavenbook tobrien]$ export MAVEN_HOME=/usr/local/maven-1.0.2
[tobrien@mavenbook tobrien]$ export PATH=${PATH}:${MAVEN_HOME}/bin
```

If Maven has been successfully installed on your machine, you should see the same output one would see on a Windows machine. Congratulations! You've installed Maven.

TIP

Some people prefer to keep local applications in a */opt* directory on Unix and a *c:\apps* directory on Windows. You can install Maven wherever you like.

What just happened?

You just installed Maven 1.0.2, and configured some environment variables. That's it! Once MAVEN_HOME is set and *maven.bat* or *maven.sh* is available on your PATH, you should be able to complete the labs in this Developer's Notebook.

What about...

…Maven 2?

It is a good time to mention Maven 2 (sometimes referred to as "m2"). Maven 2 is a complete rewrite of Maven 1. The primary goal of the rewrite is to offer a strong Java build and project comprehension API, allowing Maven to be embedded everywhere, and especially in higher-level products such as IDEs, quality tools, reporting tools, and so on. Maven 2 formalized the concept of a build lifecycle and is even easier to extend than Maven 1.

Maven 1 and 2 share a lot of concepts, but they do have several major differences. Throughout this book, we have attempted to note the differences you can expect. For more information about Maven 2, stay tuned to the Maven web site at *http://maven.apache.org/*, download the pre-release versions of Maven 2, and join the Maven user and developer mailing lists. If you've heard of Continuous Integration, you might also want to take a look at a Maven subproject named Continuum, at *http://maven.apache.org/continuum*.

Starting a New Project

Part of the hassle of setting up a new project is the amount of effort involved in creating a "development infrastructure"—automated builds, unit tests, documentation, project reporting, etc. Using Maven, you can accelerate this process by generating a skeleton project which can be used as a seed for new applications.

How do I do that?

Maven has an Application Generation plug-in (Genapp) which you can use to create a new project. Start by creating an empty *c:\dev\mavenbook\code\genapp\test-application* directory that will house the generated application. Run the Genapp plug-in by executing the genapp goal, selecting the default template, and supplying some information about your new project:

```
C:\dev\mavenbook\code\genapp\test-application>maven genapp
```

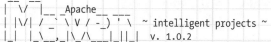

```
Attempting to download commons-jelly-tags-interaction-20030211.143817.jar.
4K downloaded
Enter a project template to use: [default]
[Enter]
Please specify an id for your application:  [app]
test-application
Please specify a name for your application:  [Example Application]
Test Application
Please specify the package for your application:  [example.app]
mdn.testapp
build:start:

genapp:
     [copy] Copying 1 file to C:\dev\mavenbook\code\genapp\test-application\
src\java\mdn\testapp
     [copy] Copying 3 files to C:\dev\mavenbook\code\genapp\test-application\
src\test\mdn\testapp
     [copy] Copying 1 file to C:\dev\mavenbook\code\genapp\test-application\
     [copy] Copying 2 files to C:\dev\mavenbook\code\genapp\test-application\
BUILD SUCCESSFUL
```

This plug-in asks the user for some input, and from this output you can
see that you are using the default application template, and you are
supplying an application ID, application name, and package for the
new project. The default application template creates a single class,
mdn.testapp.App, with a static main function and two JUnit tests.

Maven's Application Generation plug-in generated the following files and
directories:

```
test-application/
     project.properties
     project.xml
     src/
          conf/
               app.properties
          java/mdn/testapp/
               App.java
          test/mdn/testapp/
               AbstractTestCase.java
               AppTest.java
               NaughtyTest.java
```

All Maven projects have a standard directory structure which is referenced in a project's Project Object Model (POM), as described shortly. If
you have a few existing classes you want to add to a project, add them to
src/java, and if you have any unit tests add them to *src/test*. If these
existing classes and unit tests depend on any external libraries, you'll see
how to add a dependency later in this chapter. The *xdocs* directory contains project documentation in XDoc format.

project.xml is the project's descriptor; it is an XML file that contains the
POM. Let's take a look at a copy of *project.xml* which has been customized for this project:

```
<project>
  <pomVersion>3</pomVersion>
  <artifactId>test-application</artifactId>
  <name>Test Application</name>
  <currentVersion>1.0</currentVersion>

  <organization>
    <name>Your Organization</name>
    <url>http://www.someorganization.biz/</url>
    <logo>http://www.someorganization.biz/logo.gif|jpg|...</logo>
  </organization>

  <inceptionYear>2005</inceptionYear>

  <package>mdn.testapp</package>

  <logo>http://yourproject/logo.jpg|gif|...</logo>
  <description>
    An example project
  </description>

  <shortDescription>
    How to use maven in different situations
  </shortDescription>

  <!-- Many Elements Omitted (see generated POM) -->

  <dependencies/>

  <build>
    <sourceDirectory>src/java</sourceDirectory>
    <unitTestSourceDirectory>src/test</unitTestSourceDirectory>
    <unitTest>
      <includes>
        <include>**/*Test.java</include>
      </includes>
```

```
        <excludes>
          <exclude>**/NaughtyTest.java</exclude>
        </excludes>
      </unitTest>
      <resources>
        <resource>
          <directory>src/conf</directory>
          <includes>
            <include>*.properties</include>
          </includes>
        </resource>
      </resources>
    </build>
  </project>
```

This file tells Maven all about your project. The `build` element locates source code, unit tests, and resources to be packaged with your application. `name`, `artifactId`, `currentVersion`, `inceptionYear`, `description`, and `shortDescription` identify the project and provide information used to name the artifact created from this project.

Artifact? What is that? An artifact is the output of a given project. This can be a JAR, WAR, SAR, RAR, and more.

TIP

If you are working with an existing Maven project, you may see the id element in place of the artifactId element. The id element has been deprecated, and you should use artifactId instead.

The `resources` element is used by the JAR plug-in to copy resources to a JAR artifact. In this element you specify a set of resources in `resource` tags. In this example, the resources from *src/conf* will be copied to the root of the classpath. In other words, the *app.properties* resource will be copied to the root of the generated JAR artifact. If you wanted all **.properties* resources and **.xml* resources in *src/conf* to be available in the `mdn.testapp` package of the generated JAR, you would specify a `targetPath` as follows:

```
<resource>
  <directory>src/conf</directory>
  <targetPath>mdn/testapp</targetPath>
  <includes>
    <include>*.properties</include>
    <include>*.xml</include>
  </includes>
</resource>
```

project.properties lets you customize the behavior of Maven and Maven plug-ins for this project. You will be using this file later in this book to customize the look and feel of a generated web site, and the contents of a JAR file.

What about...

...Maven's ability to track information about a collaborative project?

To simplify this example, we have removed some elements from the *project.xml* file shown earlier that describe a project's mailing lists, source repository, developers, and web site. Chapters 4 and 5 go into more detail about using Maven to publish a web site and to work with an existing source code repository.

Using Maven Behind a Proxy

Maven relies on an Internet connection, and it downloads all dependencies and plug-ins over HTTP. If you are working in a corporate environment, you may need to configure Maven to work with a proxy server.

How do I do that?

You will need to set some properties in your project's *project.properties* file. The *project.properties* file allows you to customize the behavior of Maven by setting named properties. To configure a proxy server, place the following *project.properties* file in the same directory as your project's *project.xml* file:

```
maven.proxy.host = proxy.company.com
maven.proxy.port = 80
```

These properties configure Maven to connect to port 80 on the proxy.company.com machine. If you are using a proxy server that requires authentication, you will need to specify two additional properties:

```
maven.proxy.username = tobrien
maven.proxy.password = myp@ssw0rd
```

And, if you need to connect to a proxy server which requires NTLM authentication, set the following properties:

```
maven.proxy.ntlm.username = tobrien
maven.proxy.ntlm.password = myp@ssw0rd
```

Compiling and Testing a Project

You have a new project with one class and a unit test. Next, let's build the project and run the App class.

How do I do that?

Create a JAR file containing this application's classes by executing the jar:jar goal. The JAR plug-in defines a shorthand goal named jar which depends upon the jar:jar goal. Executing either goal will have the same result. All plug-ins define such a shortcut; for example, the test goal executes the test:test goal from the Test plug-in. Execute the jar goal with maven jar:

```
C:\dev\mavenbook\code\genapp\test-application>maven jar

 __ __
| \/ |__ _Apache__ ___
| |\/| / _` \ V / -_) ' \   ~ intelligent projects ~
|_|  |_\__,_|\_/\___|_||_|  v. 1.0.2

Attempting to download junit-3.8.1.jar.
118K downloaded

build:start:

java:prepare-filesystem:
    [mkdir] Created dir: C:\dev\mavenbook\code\genapp\test-application\
target\classes

java:compile:
    [echo] Compiling to C:\dev\mavenbook\code\genapp\test-application/
target/classes
    [echo]
    [javac] Compiling 1 source file to C:\dev\mavenbook\code\genapp\test-
application\target\classes

java:jar-resources:
Copying 1 file to C:\dev\mavenbook\code\genapp\test-application\target\
classes

test:prepare-filesystem:
```

```
    [mkdir] Created dir: C:\dev\mavenbook\code\genapp\test-application\
target\test-classes
    [mkdir] Created dir: C:\dev\mavenbook\code\genapp\test-application\
target\test-reports

test:test-resources:

test:compile:
    [javac] Compiling 3 source files to C:\dev\mavenbook\code\genapp\test-
application\target\test-classes

test:test:
    [junit] Running mdn.testapp.AppTest
    [junit] Tests run: 1, Failures: 0, Errors: 0, Time elapsed: 0.078 sec

jar:jar:
    [jar] Building jar: C:\dev\mavenbook\code\genapp\test-application\
target\test-application-1.0.jar
BUILD SUCCESSFUL
Total time: 9 seconds
```

Maven creates a *target* directory to hold intermediate files and JAR files.
Once the JAR has been created, execute the App class as follows:

```
C:\dev\mavenbook\code\genapp\test-application> java ^
More? target\test-application-1.0.jar mdn.testapp.App
Hello World!
```

If you want to do this again, run maven clean to remove the *target* directory and build from scratch.

What just happened?

When you ran the jar goal, Maven used the JAR plug-in to create a JAR
artifact. First, Maven figured out that it had to run a series of goals to be
able to create this application's JAR file; the JAR plug-in has a jar:jar
goal which depends on other goals which, in turn, depend on other
goals. Maven figured out that the following sequence of goals needed to
be executed: java:prepare-filesystem, java:compile, java:jar-
resources, test:prepare-filesystem, test:test-resources, test:
compile, and test:test.

Maven saw that it needed to execute a goal from the Test plug-in which
executes JUnit tests, and it checked the local Maven repository for the
JUnit JAR file. Because you haven't used Maven yet, it downloaded *junit-
3.8.1.jar* from Maven's default repository at *http://www.ibiblio.org/
maven/*. You'll learn about the local Maven repository and Maven's powerful dependency management capabilities later in this chapter.

> *What's with the ^
> and More?
> prompt? This is
> how a DOS
> command line is
> continued.*

> *Maven just works.
> The first time it
> needs to run unit
> tests it is smart
> enough to
> download JUnit
> for you if you
> don't have it
> locally. No more
> searching for JAR
> files on the Web.*

Working with the Project Object Model

The Project Object Model (POM) is a central part of Maven, and you will work with it throughout this book.

How do I do that?

The POM is also referred to as the project descriptor. The XML in *project. xml* describes a project's source code, developers, source control, licensing, as well as identifying information such as the name of the project and the name of the sponsoring organization. Maven's POM is a break with build systems of the past; instead of providing explicit instructions for each build, Maven uses a declarative approach to build management. In other words, you don't tell Maven what to do as much as Maven just knows where to look based on the contents of *project.xml*. On the other hand, Ant is an imperative approach to project builds; you end up telling Ant to compile this class, make this directory, bundle up these files into a WAR, etc. Maven maintains an assortment of plug-ins crafted to work with a standard POM—a declaration of structure, identification, and content.

If you look at the *project.xml* file generated by the previous exercise you will notice a number of elements which have been omitted from the previous discussion. The following XML lists the top-level elements in a POM, in the order in which they are expected:

```
<project>
  <extend/>
  <pomVersion/>
  <id/>
  <name/>
  <groupId/>
  <currentVersion/>
  <organization/>
  <inceptionYear/>
  <package/>
  <logo/>
  <gumpRepositoryId/>
  <description/>
  <shortDescription/>
  <url/>
  <issueTrackingUrl/>
  <siteAddress/>
  <siteDirectory/>
  <distributionSite/>
  <distributionDirectory/>
  <repository/>
  <versions/>
```

```
            <branches/>
            <mailingLists/>
            <developers/>
            <contributors/>
            <licenses/>
            <dependencies/>
            <build/>
            <reports/>
            <properties/>
        </project>
```

This chapter explores most of the elements listed in the previous XML, including contributors, developers, dependencies, reports, and repository. The labs in this chapter will provide the details, but you should use the previous XML excerpt to place elements in the proper sequence within your *project.xml* files.

Listing Available Goals

When you use Maven, you will be executing goals. A Maven plug-in is a set of related goals. For example, to create a JAR from a project, you would execute the `jar:jar` goal from the JAR plug-in as follows:

```
C:\dev\mavenbook\code\genapp> maven jar:jar
```

The `jar` before the colon separator classifies this goal as belonging to the JAR plug-in. To see a list of all the goals in the JAR plug-in, enter the following command:

```
C:\dev\mavenbook\code\genapp> maven -P jar

 __  __
|  \/  |__ _Apache__ ___
| |\/| / _` \ V / -_) ' \   ~ intelligent projects ~
|_|  |_\__,_|\_/\___|_||_|  v. 1.0.2


Goals in jar
============

[jar]                          Create the deliverable jar file.
  deploy  ..................... Deploy a jar to the remote repository
  deploy-snapshot  ............ Deploy a snapshot jar to the remote
                                repository
  install  .................... Install the jar in the local repository
  install-snapshot  ........... Install a snapshot jar in the local
                                repository
  jar  ........................ Create the deliverable jar file.
  snapshot  ................... Create a snapshot jar, ie '
                                id-YYYYMMDD.hhmmss.jar'

Plugin for creating JAR files. Requires Maven 1.0 RC2.
```

If you need to see a list of every available plug-in and goal, type the following:

```
C:\dev\mavenbook\code\genapp\test-application> maven -g | more
```

The entire list of plug-ins is a little daunting, as Maven has plug-ins for just about everything, from generating project files for different IDEs to generating WAR files to starting and stopping an application server. You will learn about some of the more useful plug-ins in the following labs.

Producing Debug Information

By now, you may have noticed that Maven is performing a good deal of heavy lifting. If you were using Ant, you would have already had to write an Ant *build.xml* file and added tasks to compile, jar, and unit test. Maven is hiding a good deal of complexity, but when debugging problems, it is nice to be able to look "behind the curtain." The ability to run Maven in debug mode and to have this tool print out every last detail of a build can be essential if you need to verify that a build is doing exactly what you think it is doing.

How do I do that?

For this lab, refer to the previous test application. When running maven test, you will receive the following output:

```
java:compile:
    [echo] Compiling to C:\dev\mavenbook\code\genapp\test-application/
target/classes
    [echo]

java:jar-resources:
    [...]
```

What is really happening during the java:compile or the java:jar-resources goals? Running maven -X test will display the full debugging output for all goals executed in a Maven build. Let's try it, and focus on the three goals listed earlier. Running maven -X test produces the following output:

```
[...]
java:compile:
    [echo] Compiling to C:\dev\mavenbook\code\genapp\test-application/
target/classes
    [javac] [DEBUG] fileset: Setup scanner in dir
        C:\dev\mavenbook\code\genapp\test-application\src\java with
        patternSet{ includes: [] excludes: [**/package.html] }
    [javac] [VERBOSE] mdn\testapp\App.java omitted as mdn/testapp/App.class
is up to date.
```

```
java:jar-resources:
[DEBUG] FileSet: Setup scanner in dir
        C:\dev\mavenbook\code\genapp\test-application\src\conf with
        patternSet{ includes: [*.properties] excludes: [] }
[VERBOSE] app.properties omitted as app.properties is up to date.
[...]
```

The output printed by the java:compile task may look familiar. It is the output of Ant's echo and javac tasks. As explained in Chapter 2, Maven frequently uses Ant tasks to perform common operations such as copying, deleting, compiling, and creating JAR files.

What just happened?

The two goals you have executed produce very simple debugging output. The java:compile goal simply scans the source directory for Java source newer than its associated class file. The java:jar-resources goal looks for resources to include in a JAR file. More complex tasks such as test:test will produce debugging information about the Virtual Machine and the class loader.

When Maven has a problem or a goal throws an exception, Maven will simply print a small error message telling you that an error occurred. If you need more information, and would like to see a stack trace, add the -e flag to your command line. With the -e flag, Maven will print a full stack trace when it encounters an error.

Adding a Dependency

You have a project with a single class which you've successfully compiled and executed. Next, you'll add a dependency to the project descriptor and start to use Maven to manage project dependencies. For the purposes of this lab, assume that you need to work with the Spring Framework. Add a dependency on two artifacts from the Spring Framework—*spring-core-1.1.4.jar* and *spring-web-1.1.4.jar*.

How do I do that?

First, you need to locate the JAR you need in Maven's default central repository, served from *ibiblio.org* at *http://www.ibiblio.org/maven/*. Load this URL in a web browser and you will see a series of directories; the directory we are interested in is *springframework*, and the structure of the subdirectories under *springframework* follows:

```
http://www.ibiblio.org/maven
    /springframework
        /jars
            spring-core-1.1.4.jar
            spring-dao-1.1.4.jar
            spring-web-1.1.4.jar
```

To depend on an artifact, you use three elements within dependency—
groupId, artifactId, and version. You can add dependencies to both
artifacts by replacing the dependencies element in *test-application/
project.xml* with the following XML:

```
<dependencies>
  <dependency>
    <groupId>springframework</groupId>
    <artifactId>spring-core</artifactId>
    <version>1.1.4</version>
  </dependency>
  <dependency>
    <groupId>springframework</groupId>
    <artifactId>spring-web</artifactId>
    <version>1.1.4</version>
  </dependency>
</dependencies>
```

Now, run the jar goal and take a look at the output of Maven; it should
contain something that looks like this:

```
Attempting to download spring-core-1.1.4.jar.
266K downloaded
Attempting to download spring-web-1.1.4.jar.
111K downloaded
```

Figure 1-1 shows the following series of events, triggered by the jar
goal:

1. Maven looked at the POM, as defined in *project.xml*, and saw the
   dependency on two artifacts in the *springframework* group. It then
   looked for *spring-core-1.1.4.jar* and *spring-web-1.1.4.jar* on your
   Maven local repository.

2. When Maven didn't find these files, it went to *http://www.ibiblio.
   org/maven/springframework/jars/* to retrieve the JARs. These JAR
   files were then downloaded and put in your Maven local repository.
   They were also added to your project's classpath. The next time your
   project asks for those files, Maven will serve them from your local
   repository.

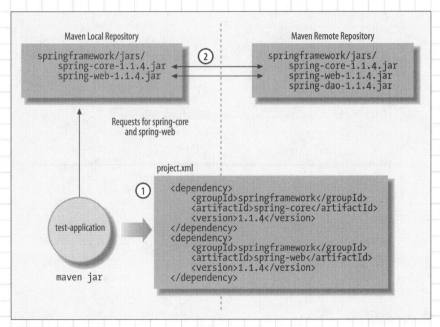

Figure 1-1. The Maven local and remote repositories serving the spring JARs for the test application project

What just happened?

Maven just saved you a serious amount of hassle and time. Prior to the arrival of Maven, dependencies were usually bundled with a project in a *lib* directory, or a project would have directions for adding the right JARs to your classpath. There are distinct advantages to managing dependencies with Maven; for starters, if your project depends on 30 external JAR files, there is no need to store multiple megabytes of JAR files in a source control repository. This means less storage space, and faster download times when you need to check a project out of source control. In addition, if you have multiple projects which depend on the same external dependency, Maven needs to download a dependency only once, and every project references a single copy of that dependency in your local Maven repository. When dependencies can be downloaded from the remote Maven repository, there is no compelling reason to store and version your project's dependencies.

When Maven downloads a dependency, it is copying a file from a remote Maven repository to a local Maven repository on your local machine. How does Maven locate a dependency? It uses the information from the dependency element in *project.xml*, as shown in Figure 1-2.

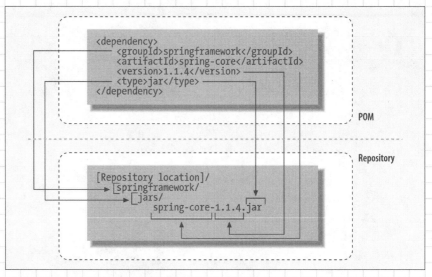

Figure 1-2. Mapping between POM and Maven repository

Specifying the `groupId` tells Maven to look in a specific directory—*springframework*. Specifying the `type` tells Maven to look in a specific subdirectory, such as *jars* or *wars* (notice the *s* that Maven is adding to the type element); in this case, `type` is omitted, as the JAR type is the default. When you specify an `artifactId`, you are telling Maven which file to download from the *jars* directory. The top-level directory, *springframework*, represents the group identifier, the first part of the JAR filename represents the artifact identifier, and the last part of the JAR filename, excluding the extension, represents the version identifier. Maven uses the following formula to resolve a dependency from a repository, where [REPO_ROOT] refers to the URL of your remote repository:

```
[REPO_ROOT]/<groupId>/<type>s/<artifactId>-<currentVersion>.<type>
```

TIP

With the introduction of Maven 2.0, the repository may start to resemble the structure of Java packages. Instead of *springframework*, a groupId in the proposed structure would be *org.springframework*. In addition, each version will have a separate directory to increase the efficiency of the Maven repository. For information on these proposed changes, see *http://docs.codehaus.org/display/MAVEN/Repository+Layout+-+Final*.

Maven handles dependencies by maintaining a local repository in your home directory. On a Unix machine, your Maven repository can be found in the *~/.maven/repository* directory, and on a Windows machine your Maven repository is in your *%USERPROFILE%* directory. If you take a look at your local Maven repository, you will notice that it now contains a directory, *springframework*. The *%USERPROFILE%\. maven\repository\springframework\jars* directory contains two files for the *spring-core* dependency: the *spring-core-1.1.4.jar* file and the *spring-core-1.1.4.jar.md5* file, which contains an MD5 hash used to verify the integrity of the *spring-core* JAR file. Maven 1 does not currently use MD5 to validate the integrity of the artifact, but future releases may use it to validate a downloaded artifact.

TIP

On a Windows machine, *%USERPROFILE%* usually resolves to a directory such as *C:\Documents and Settings\vmassol*. *%USERPROFILE%* is used in the spirit of the abbreviation for a Unix home directory.

What about...

...using the id element?

If you are working with an existing Maven project, you may have dependencies which use the id element. The following dependencies element demonstrates the use of a single id element to depend on version 1.0 of Jakarta Commons Math:

```
<dependencies>
  <dependency>
    <id>commons-math</id>
    <version>1.0</version>
  </dependency>
</dependencies>
```

Using the id element alone will work only if the groupId matches the artifactId, and if you browse the Maven repository, you will see the following directory structure:

```
/commons-math
    /jars
        commons-math-1.0.jar
        commons-math-1.1.jar
```

While a single id element will work, the use of the id tag alone is deprecated and will disappear in Maven 2. While you may see other Maven projects using this shorthand notation for dependencies, please try to use groupId and artifactId to identify your dependencies.

Depending on Snapshots

If you are developing a program that depends on a frequently changing dependency, you might want to depend on the latest build instead of hardcoding a version for each dependency. This can be especially useful when a project depends on a dependency which is still a beta of a release candidate, or if you are developing a series of interdependent Maven projects, as discussed in Chapter 3. In this lab, you'll learn how to depend on a *SNAPSHOT*.

How do I do that?

Instead of specifying a specific version in your dependency block, use the keyword SNAPSHOT as part of the version name. Every time you execute a Maven goal, Maven will check for a new version of the dependency from the remote repository. Maven will download the dependency if the remote repository has a newer version than the local repository. For example, the following dependency would always download the latest 1.2 development JAR of *spring*:

```
<dependency>
  <groupId>springframework</groupId>
  <artifactId>spring</artifactId>
  <version>1.2-SNAPSHOT</version>
</dependency>
```

What just happened?

Maven 2 increases the configurability of the SNAPSHOT dependency mechanism. The next release will allow you to specify how often Maven checks for an updated SNAPSHOT release.

When you use *SNAPSHOT* dependencies you are telling Maven to use the latest version in the remote repository. This will come in handy when you are using the Multiproject plug-in, or when you are depending on an artifact still in development, as will often be the case if you're working on a team consisting of more than a few developers. You will be using *SNAPSHOT* dependencies when your project depends on the latest development or unreleased version of a particular component. *SNAPSHOT* dependencies should be reserved for development purposes, and, as a rule, you should never release a project that depends on a *SNAPSHOT* dependency.

Performing an Offline Build

If you need to use Maven in a disconnected situation, you'll need to know how to convince Maven not to check for the presence of an up-to-date

SNAPSHOT dependency. This lab will show you how to perform an offline build using Maven.

How do I do that?

The process is simple: just use the -o command-line option. For example, if you do not have a network connection, but would like to execute the test goal, run `maven -o test`. Maven will then execute the test goal without checking for dependencies. If your project does not depend on *SNAPSHOT* builds, you should be able to disconnect your environment without having to add the -o flag. If you do rely on *SNAPSHOT* builds, you will need to use the -o flag, as Maven will attempt to check for the presence of a newer *SNAPSHOT* every time it executes a goal. In this case, the project will not build successfully without the use of the -o flag.

What about...

...performing an offline build if I haven't downloaded any artifacts?

Of course, this won't work. For an offline build to work you must already have the required dependencies in your local repository. The easiest way to get Maven to download dependencies for a project is to run a simple "noop" goal present in every Maven project—for instance, `build:start`. This goal is executed before any other goal and does not perform any action. If you run `build:start`, Maven will grab any dependency referenced from the *project.xml* file.

Using the Maven Console

If you are repeatedly running Maven from the command line, you can save yourself some time by using the Maven Console. The Maven Console provides a "shell" where you can type in the name of a goal for Maven to execute. By using the Maven Console, you can avoid waiting for the Java Virtual Machine (JVM) to start up every time you want to run a Maven goal.

How do I do that?

The Maven Console is a plug-in, and you can start it by entering `maven console` at the command prompt. This should produce the following output:

```
 __  __
|  \/  |__  _Apache__ ___
| |\/| / _` \ V / -_) ' \   ~ intelligent projects ~
|_|  |_\__,_|\_/\___|_||_|  v. 1.0.2

The following commands are available:

    list - list all available goals
    help - this message
    <goalname> - attain a goal
    quit - quits the console

test-application 1.0 >
```

At this point, you can execute any goal you could execute from the command line. Go ahead and try it; type java:compile. Maven will execute the java:compile goal and return you to the prompt to wait for another goal. To run two goals in sequence, you may enter them at the prompt, separated by a space—for example, clean test. This is known as "goal chaining" and it is a way for you to specify a series of goals you want Maven to obtain, in order. To exit the Maven Console, type quit, and to see a list of available goals, type list.

What just happened?

Maven executed the java:compile goal very quickly in the Maven Console, didn't it? When you use the Maven Console you are executing a goal in an existing JVM. When you run Maven from the command line, you have to wait for the JVM to start up every time you want to run a goal. If you are not convinced of the performance improvement, try it for yourself. Run the java:compile goal from the command line 10 times in a row, and then run the same java:compile goal from the Maven Console 10 times. Take note of the time difference, and you will see that the JVM startup time begins to increase. Use the Maven Console if you find yourself frequently running Maven goals, as it saves time by starting a JVM once.

Generating an Eclipse Project

I'll bet that you want to start working in an IDE. Maven comes with plugins for Eclipse, IntelliJ IDEA, JBuilder, JDeveloper, and Emacs. While Maven integrates well with all of these tools, this lab focuses on its integration with Eclipse, a popular open source IDE.

How do I do that?

The process is simple; just execute the `eclipse` plug-in:

```
C:\dev\mavenbook\code\genapp\test-application> maven eclipse

build:start:

eclipse:generate-project:
    [echo] Creating C:\dev\mavenbook\code\genapp\test-application/.project ...

eclipse:generate-classpath:
    [echo] Creating C:\dev\mavenbook\code\genapp\test-application/.classpath ...
    [echo] Contains JUnit tests
    [echo] Setting compile of src/test to target/test-classes
Plugin 'cactus-maven' in project 'Test Application' is not available
    [echo] Setting default output directory to target/classes

eclipse:
    [echo] Now refresh your project in Eclipse (right click on the project
and select "Refresh")
BUILD SUCCESSFUL
Total time: 2 seconds
```

Maven creates the two files which identify this project as an Eclipse project: *.project* and *.classpath*. In Eclipse, you can then import this project by following these steps:

1. Start Eclipse.

2. Select File → Import… from the menu.

3. Select Existing Project into Workspace and click the Next button.

4. Select the *C:\dev\mavenbook\code\genapp\test-application* direc- tory in the Import dialog, and click the Finish button.

You will then need to perform one more step to point Eclipse at the local Maven repository. Eclipse uses a variable named MAVEN_REPO to point to the local Maven repository. You can set MAVEN_REPO using Maven, by exe- cuting the following at the command line:

```
maven -Dmaven.eclipse.workspace=c:\eclipse\workspace eclipse:add-maven-repo
```

Executing this goal should set the global MAVEN_REPO variable in the workspace located in the *c:\eclipse\workspace* directory.

Alternatively, you can configure this variable manually by following these steps:

1. Open Eclipse preferences by selecting Window→Preferences from the menu.

2. In the tree menu on the lefthand side of the Preferences dialog, select Java → Build Path → Classpath Variables.

3. Create a new classpath variable by clicking the New button; this should bring up the New Variable Entry dialog.

4. Type `MAVEN_REPO` into the Name field.

5. Click the Folder button and select your local Maven repository.

6. Click OK and rebuild all of your projects.

You will need to configure `MAVEN_REPO` only once; this variable is global and it is shared by all Eclipse projects.

What about...

...JBuilder, JDeveloper, and IntelliJ IDEA?

All of these IDEs have simple plug-ins for Eclipse. To generate the necessary files for a JBuilder project, run `maven jbuilder`. For JDeveloper run `maven jdeveloper`, and for the IntelliJ IDEA project run `maven idea`.

Using the Eclipse Maven Plug-in

Yes, there is a quality Maven plug-in you can use in Eclipse. It supports a number of interesting features, such as the ability to edit *project.xml* files, support for Maven customization, and a Maven repository browser, among other features.

How do I do that?

Mevenide (*http://mevenide.codehaus.org/mevenide-ui-eclipse/update/index.html*) is an Eclipse plug-in which allows you to use Maven from within Eclipse. You can download it from an Eclipse Update site by following these directions:

1. Start Eclipse.

2. Select Help → Software Updates → Find and Install from the menu.

3. In the Install/Update dialog, select "Search for new feature to install," and click Next.

4. In the Install dialog, click New Remote Site.

5. In the New Update Site dialog, type `Mevenide` into the Name field, and the location of the Eclipse Update site into the URL field. The Eclipse Update site for Mevenide is *http://mevenide.codehaus.org/release/eclipse/update/site.xml*.

6. When the word *Mevenide* appears in the Install dialog, select both of the children, Maven and Mevenide, and click Next.

7. Once Maven and Mevenide are downloaded and installed, restart Eclipse.

The first thing you'll notice is that Mevenide has marked every *project. xml* file with a green icon. To open *project.xml* in the Project Object Model Editor, right-click any *project.xml* file and select Open With... → Project Object Model Editor. This editor will display the panel shown in Figure 1-3.

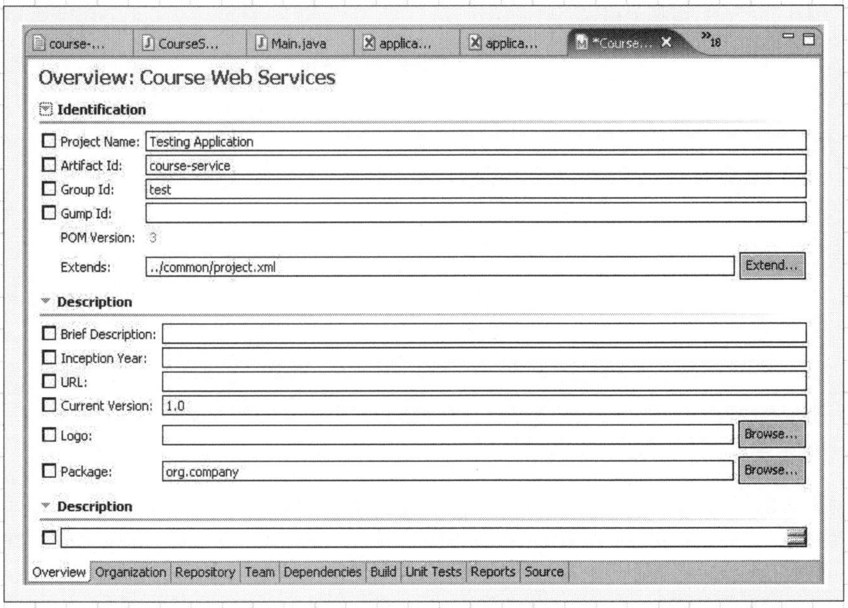

Figure 1-3. Overview panel of Mevenide's Project Object Model Editor

Mevenide provides a series of tabs which let you edit different sections of a *project.xml* file in Eclipse. As you learn more about the syntax of the *project.xml* file, know that the Mevenide Project Object Model Editor provides a GUI interface to maintaining this XML file. If you still wish to edit the XML directly, you can choose the rightmost Source tab.

In addition to a POM editor, Mevenide also provides you with a way to execute Maven goals as an Eclipse external tool. To execute a Maven goal in Eclipse, select Run → External Tools... → External Tools.... You can then create a new Maven configuration and select the desired goal from a list of every available goal. When a Maven goal is executed in Eclipse, its output is available through the Console view.

Another interesting feature of Mevenide is the Repository Browser. This tool allows you to examine the contents of a number of different remote repositories. To open the Repository Browser, select Window → Show View... → Other..., and then select Repository Browser from the Maven folder in the resulting dialog. The Repository Browser is simply a tree of every dependency in a repository, as shown in Figure 1-4, which shows dependencies for the HTTPClient and abbot groups.

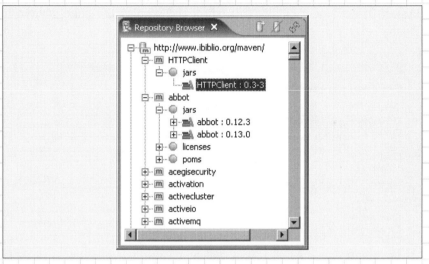

Figure 1-4. Mevenide Repository Browser view

Mevenide also provides a repository search function if you want to search the repository for a particular artifact. This can come in handy because searching *http://www.ibiblio.org/maven* for a particular dependency can be annoying. Check out Mevenide; it will save you time.

What about...

...NetBeans and JBuilder?

Support for both of these IDEs is present in the current release of Mevenide. For more details see *http://mevenide.codehaus.org/*.

...what about IntelliJ?

The IDEA plug-in maintains some goals which you can use in the same way you use the Eclipse goals. For more information, see the IDEA plug-in online documentation at *http://maven.apache.org/reference/plugins/idea/goals.html*.

Generating an Ant Build File

There are times when you will want to build using Apache Ant. Maybe your project is using an automated process which relies on Ant, or maybe you have some team members who are not yet comfortable making the transition to Maven and who wish to continue using Ant. Since many IDEs already support projects with Ant build files, you can use Maven to generate a *build.xml* file so that your project can be built using Apache Ant.

How do I do that?

Run the Ant plug-in. Running maven ant will create a *build.xml* file which contains targets to gather dependencies, build, and test your application. Take a look at the output of running the default jar target:

```
C:\dev\mavenbook\code\genapp\test-application>ant
Buildfile: build.xml

init:
    [mkdir] Created dir: C:\dev\mavenbook\code\genapp\target\lib

get-deps:
      [get] Getting: http://www.ibiblio.org/maven/springframework/jars/
spring-core-1.1.4.jar
      [get] Getting: http://www.ibiblio.org/maven/springframework/jars/
spring-web-1.1.4.jar

compile:
     [copy] Copying 1 file to C:\dev\mavenbook\code\genapp\target\classes

junit-present:
     [echo]================== WARNING =======================
     [echo] Junit isn't present in your ${ANT_HOME}/lib directory. Tests not
executed.
     [echo] =====================================================

compile-tests:

internal-test:

test:

jar:
      [jar] Building jar: C:\dev\mavenbook\code\genapp\test-application\
target\test-application-1.0.jar

BUILD SUCCESSFUL
Total time: 2 seconds
```

You may have noticed that there is a problem, and it is an illustrative problem. Apache Ant does not automatically manage the dependencies for optional Ant tasks. If you want to run the JUnit tests, you will need to copy the *junit-3.8.1.jar* file from the local Maven repository to *${ANT_HOME}/lib*. This build file contains a get-deps target which executes the Ant get task to grab all of the project's dependencies from the remote Maven repository at *http://www.ibiblio.org/maven*.

What about...

...trying to get away from Ant? Isn't Maven a replacement for Ant?

Yes and no. Ant isn't "bad," and the majority of tools still work with Ant. There is no reason not to provide interoperability with Apache Ant, and once you learn more about Jelly in Chapter 2, you'll see that Ant tasks are used extensively in Maven. Many projects use a continuous integration system which may expect an Ant build file. Running maven ant provides an easy way to continue to support these tools.

Although this is changing rapidly; many tools such as AntHill and Gump are starting to support both Ant and Maven. But, if you are still working with a tool that expects an Ant build file, run maven ant.

Migrating a Project from Ant to Maven

A fair number of projects use Ant as a build system, and you will want to migrate to Maven.

How do I do that?

Start from scratch. Create a default Maven template, and then move your code to the proper directories. Do not try to fit Maven to your own project's directories and build locations. Maven is more than a build tool; it is a standard way to think about project layout and management. If you attempt to fit Maven to your project's idea of a build, you'll end up using Maven as it was never intended. If your project consists of a complex *build.xml* file which produces a number of different deliverables, you will need to "componentize" your project and follow the model for multi-projects described in Chapter 3. You will also need to start moving your project's directory structure toward the standard Maven project directory structure presented throughout this book. In other words, don't try to "shoehorn" Maven onto your project.

If you are interested in migrating to Ant, but you don't have time to stop development, you can always use Maven to call your existing Ant targets. If you do this, you'll miss out on a large part of the benefit of using

Maven, but it is a possibility. For more information, see the informative "Migrating from Ant" document located at *http://maven.apache.org/using/migrating.html.*

What about...

...flexibility and choice?

Flexibility and choice are part of the original problem. We promise that Maven will change the way you approach building and maintaining your project, but it is important to use Maven as Maven was intended to be used. What are the differences between Maven and Ant? Where Ant offers building blocks in the form of reusable tasks such as copy, move, delete, and junit, Maven offers reusable build processes. Maven is a "build container" which allows you to reuse build processes over a series of projects. Take unit testing as just one example. With Ant, you would perform a JUnit test by including the following in your project's *build.xml* file:

```
<junit printsummary="yes" haltonfailure="yes">
  <classpath>
    <pathelement location="${build.tests}"/>
    <pathelement path="${java.class.path}"/>
  </classpath>

  <formatter type="plain"/>

  <test name="my.test.TestCase" haltonfailure="no" outfile="result">
    <formatter type="xml"/>
  </test>

  <batchtest fork="yes" todir="${reports.tests}">
    <fileset dir="${src.tests}">
      <include name="**/*Test*.java"/>
      <exclude name="**/AllTests.java"/>
    </fileset>
  </batchtest>
</junit>
```

This snippet leaves out the definition of the various paths and variables such as build.tests and java.class.path, and it also leaves out the definition of Ant targets. In addition to some sort of unit test target, you'll also need to define a target to compile the source and the unit tests, and a target to create the destination directories. Every project needs to define the same logic just to perform a unit test. To this end, most Ant projects end up using a similar directory structure, and build logic is reused by just copying and pasting target definitions into a *build.xml* file. Over time, as projects become more complex and customized, directory standards evolve and each project tends to have a different approach to compilation, testing, and packaging; over time, the *build.xml* file becomes a project in and of itself. The larger your custom Ant build file is the more entropy creeps into your build process. Ant is less a build tool than it is a language which provides a build-specific API. While Ant 1.6 has Ant libraries and macros, Ant is still a long way from achieving the global reusability present in Maven.

With Maven, the Test plug-in defines logic common to all projects which need to compile and execute unit tests. The Test plug-in has captured best practices for compiling and executing unit tests, and it has made these best practices available to all projects. When you run `maven test`, Maven passes information from the POM to the Test plug-in, and the Test plug-in depends on a goal from the Java plug-in to perform the compilation. Nowhere in a Maven project are you explicitly telling the build container how to execute a JUnit test. If you were, you would be running into the same problem you faced in Ant. Just as you are not telling a `Servlet` container how to unpack your WAR file, you are not telling Maven how to build your project. Maven is a build container. It provides an abstraction layer to separate build logic from projects. Many people are initially attracted to Maven because it provides dependency management, but the main benefit of Maven is that it provides a standard development infrastructure across multiple projects. Dependency management is simply a byproduct of a standard development infrastructure.

TIP

Maven provides a development infrastructure and a uniform project layout, and to this end you should try to let Maven take care of most of the build process details. Instead of spending your valuable time writing build scripts, use Maven plug-ins and focus on writing your application.

The following chapters will show you how to tweak and customize Maven, but you need to make sure that you are not asking Maven to be another Ant. It is entirely possible to have one huge Maven project with a large *maven.xml* file full of Jelly script (see Chapter 2) that re-creates Ant's *build.xml* file, but if you do that *you've missed the point of Maven entirely*. If you find yourself including a great deal of build-related logic in your Maven build, you need to rethink your usage of Maven. A highly customized Maven build is an oxymoron; your Maven projects should leverage the existing plug-ins where possible. For example, if your project needs to compile Java source code and create a JAR file, use the

Java plug-in and the JAR plug-in. If you ignore reuse through Maven's plug-ins and use Maven's Ant integration to reinvent wheels, you're better off not using Maven at all. Don't misuse Maven; use this tool as it was intended, and save yourself the bile.

Vincent says, "Neo, take the red pill..." and Tim says, "Resistance is futile."

Generating Project Documentation

If you are developing a Java application or library, you might want to generate JavaDoc.

How do I do that?

Simply execute the javadoc goal and Maven will generate project documentation. Here is the output of the execution of the javadoc goal:

```
C:\dev\mavenbook\code\genapp\test-application>maven javadoc

  __  __
|  \/  |__ _Apache__ ___
| |\/| / _` \ V / -_) ' \   ~ intelligent projects ~
|_|  |_\__,_|\_/\___|_||_|   v. 1.0.2

build:start:

xdoc:init:

maven-javadoc-plugin:report:
    [mkdir] Created dir: C:\dev\mavenbook\code\genapp\test-application\
target\javadoc\src
    [javadoc] Generating Javadoc
    [javadoc] Javadoc execution
    [javadoc] Loading source files for package mdn.testapp...
    [javadoc] Constructing Javadoc information...
    [javadoc] Standard Doclet version 1.5.0_01
    [javadoc] Building tree for all the packages and classes...
    [javadoc] Generating C:\dev\mavenbook\code\genapp\test-application\
target\docs\apidocs\constant-values.html...
    [javadoc] Copying file C:\Documents and Settings\tobrien\.maven\cache\
maven-javadoc-plugin-1.7\plugin-resources\stylesheet.css to file C:\dev\
mavenbook\code\genapp\test-application\target\docs\apidocs\stylesheet.css...
    [javadoc] Building index for all the packages and classes...
    [javadoc] Building index for all classes...
    [delete] Deleting directory C:\dev\mavenbook\code\genapp\test-
application\target\javadoc\src
BUILD SUCCESSFUL
Total time: 7 seconds
```

Once this goal has been executed, JavaDoc is available in *test-application/target/javadoc/src*.

What just happened?

Once again, Maven did all of the heavy lifting. You wanted JavaDoc, you told Maven to generate JavaDoc, end of story. Note that you didn't need to tell Maven anything about the project; it just "knew" what to do. Much of Maven is this straightforward; after you tell Maven about your project there isn't much more you need to do. It handles the details.

Telling Maven About Your Team

Maven is a great collaboration tool which you can use to generate developer activity reports, as well as lists of project contributors and mailing lists.

How do I do that?

Most projects have a mailing list which is used to discuss architecture and implementation. And, from one perspective, projects such as Tomcat, Maven, and Ant are nothing more than a community of developers who share a subscription to the same mailing list. Mailing lists are not just for open source projects; many organizations are starting to use the same collaborative model used in open, public development. Because mailing lists are a pivotal part of collaboration, Maven provides a way for you to specify project mailing lists in *project.xml*. The following excerpt from *project.xml* adds a `mailingLists` element:

```
<mailingLists>
  <mailingList>
    <name>Maven User List</name>
    <subscribe>users-subscribe@maven.apache.org</subscribe>
    <unsubscribe>users-unsubscribe@maven.apache.org</unsubscribe>
    <archive>http://marc.theaimsgroup.com/?l=turbine-maven-user</archive>
  </mailingList>
  <mailingList>
    <name>Maven Developer List</name>
    <subscribe>dev-subscribe@maven.apache.org</subscribe>
    <unsubscribe>dev-unsubscribe@maven.apache.org</unsubscribe>
    <archive>http://marc.theaimsgroup.com/?l=turbine-maven-dev</archive>
  </mailingList>
</mailingLists>
```

There are two types of team members in Maven projects: contributors and developers. While the definition may change for your project, contributors are usually members of an open source community who have contributed patches or documents, and developers are core members of a project. In the ASF, contributors and committers can both contribute to a

project, but contributors have neither write access to the source repository nor a vote in major project decisions. The following excerpt from
project.xml adds a `contributor` and a `developer` element to *project.xml*:

```
<developers>
  <developer>
    <name>Vincent Massol</name>
    <id>vmassol</id>
    <email>vmassol@apache.org</email>
    <organization>Apache Software Foundation</organization>
    <roles>
       <role>Author</role>
       <role>Developer</role>
    </roles>
    <url>http://www.massol.net</url>
    <timezone>+1</timezone>
  </developer>
</developers>
<contributors>
  <contributor>
    <name>Tim OBrien</name>
    <email>tobrien@apache.org</email>
    <organization>Apache Software Foundation</organization>
    <roles>
       <role>Author</role>
       <role>Developer</role>
    </roles>
    <url>http://www.oreillynet.com/pub/au/1738</url>
    <timezone>-6</timezone>
  </contributor>
</contributors>
```

What just happened?

You told Maven who is working on a project, and this will come in handy
once we've generated a project web site. The developer and contributor
information listed in this POM is used by the site generation plug-in, and
a number of plug-ins that generate reports from source control. Speaking
of source control…

Pointing Maven at Source Control

Do you use source control? Tell Maven about it, and you'll be able to
generate some interesting reports described later in this book. Once you
have associated your project with a source code repository, you will be
able to use the Maven Source Control Management (SCM) plug-in which

provides goals for updating and releasing from a version control system such as CVS or Subversion.

How do I do that?

You need to add a repository element to your project's *project.xml*. The following repository element is from the Apache Struts project, and it points to the Subversion repository available at *http://svn.apache.org/repos/asf/struts/core/trunk*:

```
<repository>
  <connection>
    scm:svn:http://svn.apache.org/repos/asf/struts/core/trunk
  </connection>
  <developerConnection>
    scm:svn:https://svn.apache.org/repos/asf/struts/core/trunk
  </developerConnection>
  <url>http://svn.apache.org/repos/asf/struts/core/trunk</url>
</repository>
```

The connection element tells Maven about the read-only location of the SCM. scm identifies this URL as being an SCM location, svn tells Maven that this URL will be for a Subversion repository, and the final section of the URL is the location to the project's trunk. You may also specify the developerConnection; you use this element when you need to segment your audience into people without write access to source code, and people with write access.

The url element supplies a URL that can be used to browse the repository. In the case of Struts, they have elected to point to the Subversion repository itself, as it can be browsed with a regular web browser. The Struts team could also elect to point to the ViewCVS instance configured to point to the ASF Subversion repository, which can be found at the following URL: *http://cvs.apache.org/viewcvs.cgi/struts/core/trunk/?root=Apache-SVN*.

When you point a *project.xml* file at a particular source control system, you can also specify the different versions and branches of a particular project. The following XML shows a reduced version of the versions and branches elements from the Apache Struts *project.xml* file:

```
<versions>
  <version>
    <id>1.2.0</id>
    <name>1.2.0</name>
    <tag>STRUTS_1_2_0</tag>
  </version>
  <version>
    <id>1.2.6</id>
    <name>1.2.6</name>
```

```
        <tag>STRUTS_1_2_6</tag>
      </version>
    </versions>

    <branches>
      <branch>
        <tag>STRUTS_1_1_BRANCH</tag>
      </branch>
      <branch>
        <tag>STRUTS_1_2_BRANCH</tag>
      </branch>
    </branches>
```

Versions are used by several plug-ins, such as the Announcements plug-in, which is used to create release notes for each version.

What about...

...CVS?

While many corporate and open source projects have switched to Sub-version, some major open source projects such as JBoss have yet to make the jump to Subversion. If your project is using CVS, you will need to add a repository element similar to the repository element from the Jakarta Cactus project shown here:

```
<repository>
  <connection>
    scm:cvs:pserver:anoncvs@cvs.apache.org:/home/cvspublic:jakarta-cactus
  </connection>
  <url>http://cvs.apache.org/viewcvs.cgi/jakarta-cactus/</url>
</repository>
```

The previous excerpt is appropriate if you are exposing your repository using CVS pserver. If you are accessing CVS over SSH, you will need to set your CVS_RSH environment variable to ssh and use the following syntax:

```
<repository>
  <connection>
    scm:cvs:pserver:anoncvs@cvs.apache.org:/home/cvspublic:jakarta-cactus
  </connection>
  <url>http://cvs.apache.org/viewcvs.cgi/jakarta-cactus/</url>
  <developerConnection>
    scm:cvs:ext:tobrien@somehost:/home/cvs/repository:modulename
  </developerConnection>
</repository>
```

Creating a Project Web Site

Maven can create a project web page, with metrics and information about a project.

How do I do that?

To create a Maven project web site, use the Site plug-in by running the following Maven goal:

```
C:\dev\mavenbook\code\genapp\test-application> maven site
```

Running the Site plug-in will create the project's web site in the default site output directory: *test-application/target/docs/index.html*. If you load this HTML, you will see a site with a distinctive Maven look and feel. Figure 1-5 shows a sample of a lightly customized Maven web site complete with a custom organization logo and project logo. Instead of showing you a contrived web site, you can see the site of a project currently using Maven as a build system—Jaxen.

Figure 1-5. Sample Maven project web site

Most Maven sites have a Project Documentation navigation section which provides links to information common to all Maven projects. Project Info contains information about the project, a list of the project mailing lists, and information about source control and issue tracking (you'll discover all this in Chapter 4). Content for the generated Maven web site is developed by creating and modifying XML markup in the *xdocs* directory. In Figure 1-5, the project contains five project-specific documents: Overview, FAQ, Releases, CVS Access, and Status. These documents are included in the left navigation bar because they are included in the *xdocs/navigation.xml* file. The *xdocs* directory is where Maven stores project-specific documentation in an XML XDoc format. Here are the contents of the *navigation.xml* document for Jaxen:

```
<?xml version="1.0" encoding="ISO-8859-1"?>

<project name="jaxen" repository="jaxen" href="http://jaxen.org">

    <title>jaxen: universal java xpath engine</title>

    <body>
      <links>
        <item name="The Werken Company" href="http://www.werken.com/"/>
      </links>
      <menu name="jaxen">
        <item name="Overview" href="/index.html"/>
        <item name="FAQ" href="/faq.html"/>
        <item name="Releases" href="/releases.html"/>
        <item name="CVS Access" href="/cvs-usage.html"/>
        <item name="Status" href="/status.html"/>
      </menu>
    </body>

</project>
```

The `links` element puts a link to *http://www.werken.com* on the righthand side of the page, under the project logo, and the `menu` element contains items to appear in the lefthand navigation area. One of the files in the menu is *xdocs/index.xml*. Here are the abbreviated contents of the *xdocs/index.xml* file from Jaxen:

```
<?xml version="1.0"?>
<document url="http://jaxen.org/index.xml">

    <properties>
      <author email="bob@eng.werken.com">bob mcwhirter</author>
      <title>jaxen</title>
    </properties>

    <body>
      <section name="News">
        <p>
          Added the slidedeck from my
          <a href="/pdf/intro-slides.pdf">SD-West presentation</a>.
        </p>
        <p>
```

```
                    Check out these
                    <a href="http://dom4j.org/benchmarks/xpath/index.html">Performance
                    Benchmarks</a> comparing dom4j and Jaxen against Xerces and Xalan.
                </p>
            </section>
        [...]
        </document>
```

Once you've generated your project site, load *target/docs/index.html* in a browser to see your project's web site.

What about...

...the syntax of these files?

You can find more information about the syntax and format of the *navigation.xml* file in the Maven XDoc Plug-in FAQ (*http://maven.apache. org/reference/plugins/xdoc/faq.html*), and you can find more information about the format of individual pages at the Maven XDoc Plug-in page (*http://maven.apache.org/reference/plugins/xdoc/index.html*). This plug-in page also contains more instructions for customizing the output and behavior of the site generation plug-in.

See Chapter 4 for a more in-depth analysis of the various reports that can shed light on project activity and structure.

Customizing Site Reports

Site generation creates a number of useful reports, but depending on your style, you may want to deactivate some of these reports.

How do I do that?

To change the reports generated by Maven's site generation, alter the contents of the reports element in *project.xml*. Here is a reports element with several available reports activated:

```
<reports>
    <report>maven-changelog-plugin</report>
    <report>maven-changes-plugin</report>
    <report>maven-checkstyle-plugin</report>
    <report>maven-clover-plugin</report>
    <report>maven-cruisecontrol-plugin</report>
    <report>maven-developer-activity-plugin</report>
    <report>maven-faq-plugin</report>
    <report>maven-file-activity-plugin</report>
    <report>maven-license-plugin</report>
    <report>maven-linkcheck-plugin</report>
```

```
        <report>maven-javadoc-plugin</report>
        <report>maven-jdepend-plugin</report>
        <report>maven-jira-plugin</report>
        <report>maven-junit-report-plugin</report>
        <report>maven-jxr-plugin</report>
        <report>maven-pmd-plugin</report>
        <report>maven-simian-plugin</report>
        <report>maven-tasklist-plugin</report>
    </reports>
```

To exclude a report from Maven's site generation, just remove the report's plug-in element from the `reports` element. A Maven project that does not specify the `reports` element generates a set of default reports: jdepend, Checkstyle, changes, changelog, developer-activity, file-activity, license, javadoc, jxr, junit, linkcheck, and tasklist. When you add a `reports` element to your project's *project.xml* file, you must list all reports you wish to have generated.

What just happened?

The `reports` element lists all these fancy reports, but you probably want to know what all of these reports provide. Table 1-1 provides a brief description of some of these reports.

Table 1-1. Report plug-ins

Report plug-in	Description
maven-changelog-plugin	Changelog is a plug-in that uses the repository element to create a report of recent changes in source control.
maven-changes-plugin	Formats a *changes.xml* document in *xdocs*.
maven-checkstyle-plugin	Reports on the style of your Java code.
maven-clover-plugin	Uses a commercial test coverage tool to generate an HTML of you project's unit test coverage.
maven-cruisecontrol-plugin	This plug-in is discussed in Chapter 4.
maven-developer-activity-plugin	Creates a report of recent source control activity, by developer.
maven-faq-plugin	Formats project FAQ documents from *xdocs*.
maven-file-activity-plugin	Creates a report of recent source control activity, by file.
maven-findbugs-plugin	Finds common bug patterns in Java code.
maven-license-plugin	Includes a link to the project's license in the project reports.
maven-linkcheck-plugin	Tests all links in the generated site and creates a report listing 404s.
maven-javadoc-plugin	Adds JavaDoc to the generate Maven site.

Table 1-1. Report plug-ins (continued)

Report plug-in	Description
maven-jcoverage-plugin	Generates reports and graphs about unit test coverage.
maven-jdepend-plugin	Creates a report which lists dependencies between packages.
maven-jira-plugin	Reads open issues from a commercial issue-tracking system known as Jira, and creates a report.
maven-junit-report-plugin	Creates a report that aggregates JUnit results.
maven-jxr-plugin	Creates an annotated cross-reference of Java Source.
maven-pmd-plugin	Generates a report of potential coding issues such as unused local variables and complicated expressions.
maven-simian-plugin	Finds duplicative source code throughout the source tree.
maven-statcvs-plugin	Generates statistics and graphs of CVS activity.
maven-tasklist-plugin	Scans for @todo tags in source.

For a more comprehensive list of plug-ins and reports, see:

- Maven plug-ins: *http://maven.apache.org/reference/plugins/index.html*
- Maven plug-in Sandbox: *http://maven.apache.org/plugins-sandbox/index.html*
- Maven plug-ins hosted at SourceForge: *http://maven-plugins.sourceforge.net/*
- Third-party Maven plug-ins: *http://maven.apache.org/reference/3rdparty.html*

CHAPTER 2

Customizing Maven

In Chapter 1 you worked with the *project.xml* file, which describes the project, organization, team, location of source files, and other information Maven uses to build a project. You saw how to list available goals, and how easy it is to start using Maven. Often you'll need to customize the build process Maven uses to suit your own needs; for example, you may need to copy a JAR file to another directory, or you may want to write your own goal. This chapter focuses on Jelly and the *maven.xml* file.

When customizing Maven, you make use of an XML scripting language called *Jelly*. Jelly is a series of XML tags, executed sequentially; Jelly tags are grouped into tag libraries, and a series of core tags provide basic control structures and loops. If you are familiar with an Ant's build file, Jelly will make sense to you. In the context of Maven, Jelly is used as a scripting language, and Maven 1 plug-ins are written mostly in Jelly. This chapter focuses on how to use Jelly to extend and customize Maven.

TIP

While Maven 1 plug-ins are written in Jelly, Maven 2 moves away from this XML scripting language in favor of plug-ins written in Java (plain old Java). So, don't get too enamored with Jelly. Maven 2 is moving away from Jelly for a number of reasons, one of them being performance. As a consequence, always try to reduce the size of your *maven.xml* file and reuse the existing plug-ins as much as possible. This will save you countless hours when you switch to Maven 2 in the future. After telling you this, why should you still read this chapter? Because you need to know Jelly for Maven 1, and Maven 2 will still support it in some fashion, but plug-in developers will be encouraged to write plug-ins in Java. Maven 2 may also include integration with other Java scripting frameworks, such as Groovy and Marmalade. This chapter isn't just about Jelly, and many of the concepts presented in this chapter will remain relevant.

The sample project, called Weather, which is used in this lab, is available from the *http://www.mavenbook.org* web site. You can also check out the Weather project from a Subversion repository at *http://www. mavenbook.org/svn/mdn/code/*.

Installing a Plug-in from a Remote Repository

All your Java buddies are using the latest and greatest version of some fancy Maven plug-in, and you are starting to feel left out and ignored. How did they get the plug-in? And once they obtained it, how did they install it? To demonstrate the process of installing a plug-in, install the Apache Axis plug-in in your Maven installation.

How do I do that?

The first thing you need to know is the location of the Maven remote repository where the plug-in you wish to install is located. In the case of the Apache Axis plug-in, the repository is at *http://maven-plugins. sourceforge.net/maven/*. However, this repository is synced every few hours to the ibiblio repository at *http://www.ibiblio.org/maven/*. The ibiblio repository is the default Maven remote repository and the one that will be used if you don't tell Maven otherwise. Should you still wish to add the *remote* repository to your Maven configuration, you should modify your *build.properties* file (or *project.properties* file if you want to share the settings with others) and include the following property:

```
maven.repo.remote=http://www.ibiblio.org,http://maven-plugins.sf.net/maven
```

However, as this repository is synced with ibiblio, it's not necessary for installing the Axis plug-in. At the time of this writing, the latest version of the Axis plug-in (as can be seen at *http://www.ibiblio.org/maven/ maven-plugins/plugins/*) is version 0.7. To install it, you need to use the plugin:download goal of the Plugin plug-in, passing it some properties, as shown shortly.

In the same manner you define a groupId, an artifactId, and a version when you create a dependency in your *project.xml* file, you need to pass the same properties to the Plugin plug-in so that it knows the exact location of the plug-in you want to download and install. Issue the following command from any directory to install version 0.7 of the Axis plug-in:

```
C:\>maven plugin:download -DgroupId=maven-plugins ^
More? -DartifactId=maven-axis-plugin -Dversion=0.7
```

```
 __  __
|  \/  |__ _Apache__  ___
| |\/| / _` \ V / -_) ' \   ~ intelligent projects ~
|_|  |_\__,_|\_/\___|_||_|   v. 1.0.2

build:start:

plugin:download-artifact:
    [echo] repo is 'http://www.ibiblio.org/maven'
    [echo] trying to download http://www.ibiblio.org/maven/maven-plugins/
plugins/maven-axis-plugin-0.7.jar
11K downloaded

plugin:download:
    [copy] Copying 1 file to C:\apps\maven-1.0.2\plugins
BUILD SUCCESSFUL
Total time: 2 seconds
```

You may wonder how to extract the `groupId`, `artifactId`, and `version` information from the plug-in URL. Figure 2-1 shows how to perform this mapping for the Axis plug-in.

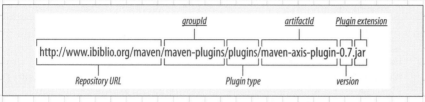

Figure 2-1. Convention for locating a plug-in in remote repository

---

TIP

To find the location of the plug-in to download, use:

        [repository URL]/[groupId]/plugins/[artifactId]-[version].jar

This is the general "formula" used by the Plugin plug-in.

Note that you can also run the `plugin:download` goal in interactive mode by simply executing the `plugin:download` goal with no options:

```
C:\>maven plugin:download

 __  __
|  \/  |__ _Apache__  ___
| |\/| / _` \ V / -_) ' \   ~ intelligent projects ~
|_|  |_\__,_|\_/\___|_||_|   v. 1.0.2

What is the artifactId of the plugin to download (e.g. maven-axis-plugin)?
maven-axis-plugin
What is the groupId of the plugin to download? [maven]
maven-plugins
```

In Maven 2, plug-
ins will be
downloaded on
demand. The
first time a plug-
in is used, it will
be downloaded
from a remote
repository.

```
What is the version of the plugin to download?
0.7
build:start:

plugin:download-artifact:
    [echo] repo is 'http://www.ibiblio.org/maven'
    [echo] trying to download http://www.ibiblio.org/maven/maven-plugins/
plugins/maven-axis-plugin-0.7.jar
11K downloaded

plugin:download:
    [copy] Copying 1 file to C:\apps\maven-1.0.2\plugins
BUILD SUCCESSFUL
Total time: 33 seconds
```

In order to verify that the plug-in has been installed successfully, try listing its goals by typing maven -P axis. You should see a list of goals
available in the Axis plug-in.

To check that the correct version of the plug-in is installed (version 0.7
for this lab), type maven -i:

```
C:\>maven -i

[...]
maven-aspectj-plugin-3.2
maven-aspectwerkz-plugin-1.2
maven-axis-plugin-0.7
maven-caller-plugin-1.1
maven-castor-plugin-1.2 [...]
```

That's it! The Axis plug-in is installed and available, and all you had to
do was execute the plugin:download goal.

What about...

...the other Maven remote repositories?

At the time of this writing, there are several well-known public Maven
remote repositories that are automatically synced with the main ibiblio
repository:

- The Apache repository
- The Maven-Plugins repository
- The Codehaus repository
- And several others (including OSJava, OpenSymphony, and MortBay)

If you are using the main ibiblio repository there is no reason to add
these repositories to your own list of remote repositories, as they all
serve as sources for the default repository.

Customizing Plug-in Behavior

In this lab, you'll be working with a web service maintained by the U.S. government's National Oceanic and Atmospheric Administration (NOAA). The U.S. government recently decided that weather feeds should be made available to the general public at no charge, so now it provides a forecast server at *http://weather.gov/xml/*. You are going to use the Maven Axis plug-in to generate classes which will retrieve a forecast from this web service. To do this, you will need to customize the behavior of the Axis plug-in.

How do I do that?

If you've successfully installed the Axis plug-in, `maven -P axis` should list the goals available in the plug-in; one of them should be `axis:wsdl2java`. You are going to use this goal to generate a client library from the Web Service Description Language (WSDL) for the weather web service.

You can find the WSDL for the NOAA forecast service at *http://weather. gov/forecasts/xml/DWMLgen/wsdl/ndfdXML.wsdl*. A *WSDL document* is an XML document which completely describes the methods available in a SOAP service. The Axis plug-in is going to use this XML document to create a client library. For the purposes of this lab, this WSDL document is stored in *weather/src/wsdl/weather.wsdl*. The Axis plug-in will generate Java source files for all WSDL documents found in this directory.

To use the output of the Axis plug-in, your project will need to include the following dependencies:

```
<dependency>
  <groupId>commons-discovery</groupId>
  <artifactId>commons-discovery</artifactId>
  <version>20030211.213356</version>
</dependency>
<dependency>
  <groupId>commons-logging</groupId>
  <artifactId>commons-logging</artifactId>
  <version>1.0.4</version>
</dependency>
<dependency>
  <groupId>axis</groupId>
  <artifactId>axis</artifactId>
  <version>1.2-RC3</version>
</dependency>
<dependency>
  <groupId>axis</groupId>
  <artifactId>axis-jaxrpc</artifactId>
  <version>1.2-RC3</version>
</dependency>
```

```
<dependency>
  <groupId>axis</groupId>
  <artifactId>axis-saaj</artifactId>
  <version>1.2-RC3</version>
</dependency>
<dependency>
  <groupId>axis</groupId>
  <artifactId>axis-wsdl4j</artifactId>
  <version>1.2-RC3</version>
</dependency>
```

To generate this client library, you will need to configure the Axis plug-in to generate client-side bindings from the WSDL document. And to do this, you will need to set the values of plug-in properties in your *project. properties* file. There are two places where you can discover the properties a plug-in exposes: the plug-in project web site and your local plug-in cache. To find a plug-in's properties from your local cache, take a look at the *~/.maven/cache/maven-axis-plugin-0.7/plugin.properties* file. It should contain the following:

```
maven.axis.dir=${maven.build.dir}/axis
maven.axis.generated.dir=${maven.axis.dir}/src
maven.axis.test.dir=${maven.axis.dir}/test
maven.axis.url=${maven.src.dir}/wsdl
maven.axis.all=true
maven.axis.deployscope=session
maven.axis.factory=org.apache.axis.wsdl.toJava.JavaGeneratorFactory
maven.axis.helpergen=false
maven.axis.serverside=true
maven.axis.skeletondeploy=true
maven.axis.noimports=no
maven.axis.verbose=yes
maven.axis.debug=false
maven.axis.typemappingversion=1.1
maven.axis.timeout=45000
```

This file lists the default values for the plug-in's properties, and in this case you can see that the maven.axis.serverside variable is set to true by default. Since you are going to be generating client-side bindings, this variable needs to be set to false for this project. You will also notice that the value of maven.axis.timeout is set to 45000 milliseconds; in this project, you will set the timeout to 20 seconds. For a friendlier list of the Axis plug-in properties, see the plug-in web site at *http://maven-plugins. sourceforge.net/maven-axis-plugin/properties.html*. To customize the behavior of this plug-in, place the following in your *weather/project. properties* file:

```
#Maven XDoc Plug-in Customization
maven.xdoc.date = left
maven.xdoc.date.format = MM/dd/yyyy
```

```
# Maven Axis Plug-in Customization
maven.axis.serverside = false
maven.axis.timeout = 20000
# Maven Test Plug-in Customization
maven.test.skip = false
maven.test.fork = yes
```

Now, when you run the axis:wsdl2java goal, it creates a client library with a 20-second timeout. You will also notice that the *project.properties* file customizes the behavior of two other plug-ins: Test and XDoc. Later in this chapter you will see how to customize the XDoc plug-in.

Running maven axis:wsdl2java will create the client library for this SOAP service, and will store the generated source in maven.axis.generate.dir. You should also be able to run unit tests in the sample project to see that the project has a unit test to verify the operation of the NOAA forecast web service.

Writing a Custom Goal

To generate a client library for a SOAP service, you need to download the WSDL you are going to pass to wsdl2java. Define a custom goal—weather:get-wsdl—to download the service description from NOAA.

How do I do that?

To write your own goal, add some Jelly script to the *weather/maven.xml* file. Here's a simple custom goal that retrieves a WSDL document with Ant's get task. The custom goal is defined as follows:

```
<?xml version="1.0" encoding="UTF-8"?>

<project xmlns:j="jelly:core" xmlns:ant="jelly:ant"
    xmlns:maven="jelly:maven" default="jar">

  <goal name="weather:get-wsdl" description="Retrieves WSDL document">
    <j:set var="wsdl"
        value="http://weather.gov/forecasts/xml/DWMLgen/wsdl/ndfdXML.wsdl"/>
    <ant:echo>Retrieving WSDL from ${wsdl}</ant:echo>
    <ant:get src="${wsdl}" dest="${basedir}/src/wsdl/weather.wsdl"/>
  </goal>

</project>
```

In your project, the URL of the WSDL document should be defined in project.properties. This will make configuration much easier.

The value of the ${wsdl} property is set with j:set, a message is printed to the console, and the document is retrieved and saved to *weather/src/wsdl*. This script uses the echo task from Apache Ant to print out a message, and you can run it from the command line with maven weather: get-wsdl, which produces the following output:

```
C:\dev\mavenbook\code\weather>maven weather:get-wsdl

 __  __
|  \/  |__ _Apache__ ___
| |\/| / _` \ V / -_) ' \   ~ intelligent projects ~
|_|  |_\__,_|\_/\___|_||_|  v. 1.0.2

build:start:

weather:get-wsdl:
    [echo] Retrieving WSDL from http://weather.gov/forecasts/xml/DWMLgen/
wsdl/ndfdXML.wsdl
    [get] Getting: http://weather.gov/forecasts/xml/DWMLgen/wsdl/ndfdXML.
wsdl
BUILD SUCCESSFUL
Total time: 2 seconds
```

What just happened?

The j:set tag sets the wsdl property to the URL from which you are
retrieving the WSDL document. When you set this variable, it is made
available to the Jelly script and can be referenced with ${wsdl}. The set
tag comes from the core Jelly tag library, which contains tags to allow
you to set variables, perform conditional tests, and iterate over collec-
tions. This chapter is going to explore a few tags from the core Jelly tag
library, such as j:if and j:forEach. For more information about Jelly's
core tag library, see *http://jakarta.apache.org/commons/jelly/tags.html*.

The *maven.xml* file uses XML namespaces to identify tag libraries used in
this Jelly script, and in this XML document the ant prefix is mapped to
the jelly:ant namespace. The jelly:ant namespace maps directly to
the Jelly Ant tag library, which allows you to call any Ant task from a
Jelly script. In this task we've used Ant's echo task as it would appear in
an Ant *build.xml* file:

```
<ant:echo>Print out some important message!</ant:echo>
```

The Ant task element needs to be associated with the jelly:ant
namespace. This takes some getting used to, but rest assured, you can do
anything in a custom Maven goal that you can do in an Ant build script.
You can use any other Ant tasks you are familiar with; take a look at the
following Maven goal from another *maven.xml* file:

```
<goal name="zipsource" prereqs="java:compile">
  <ant:copy todir="${basedir}/target/src">
    <ant:fileset dir="${basedir}/src/main/java">
      <ant:include name="**/*.java"/>
    </ant:fileset>
  </ant:copy>
  <ant:zip destfile="${basedir}/target/source.zip">
    <ant:fileset dir="${basedir}/target/src"/>
  </ant:zip>
</goal>
```

Any Ant task you can use in a *build.xml* file can be used in a Jelly script. There's a comprehensive list of Ant tasks in Ant's online manual, at *http://ant.apache.org/manual/index.html*. Actually, the `jelly:ant` namespace is bound by default. Instead of using `ant:copy` or `ant:include`, you can just type `copy` or `include` if you find that more convenient. Even though you may save yourself time by omitting the `ant` namespace prefix, you are encouraged to use it. There is nothing particularly special about Ant, and giving it a default namespace binding is somewhat arbitrary. There is a good chance that this default binding may be removed in future versions of Maven. Always use the `ant` namespace prefix in Jelly.

What about...

...Maven being a replacement for Ant?

This isn't exactly true. Maven is not a "replacement" for Ant as much as it builds upon the success of systems such as Ant. While Ant provides projects with an XML build script, Maven is a build container. Many Maven plug-ins are built on Apache Ant tasks; in this way, Maven 1 reuses Apache Ant.

Defining a preGoal

Since you would like to incorporate the generated SOAP client into your own project, you need to use the Maven Axis plug-in. When the Axis plug-in generates source, your build needs to make sure that the source it generates is included in your project's compilation. To accomplish this, you need to define a `preGoal` and `postGoal` on the `java:compile` goal.

How do I do that?

The Axis plug-in generates source files and places them in `maven.axis.generated.dir`, which defaults to *target/axis/src*. While you don't want to copy the generated source files to your project by copying them to *src/main/java*, you do want these files to be included in your project's artifact. You need to execute the `axis:compile` goal before you execute the `java:compile` goal, as `axis:compile` will add the source generated by `axis:wsdl2java` to the compilation source path. The following *maven.xml* file uses a `preGoal` which executes another goal before `java:compile`:

```
<?xml version="1.0" encoding="UTF-8"?>

<project default="jar"
    xmlns:j="jelly:core"
    xmlns:ant="jelly:ant"
    xmlns:maven="jelly:maven"
```

Maven 2 gets rid of preGoal and postGoal. In Maven 2 a build is defined as a series of phases, such as build, compile, and test. Specific goals bind to phases in a project's build lifecycle.

```
<preGoal name="java:compile">
  <attainGoal name="axis:compile" />
</preGoal>
</project>
```

Executing the `java:compile` goal produces the following output (some file paths have been truncated):

```
 __ __ __
|  \/  |__ _Apache__ _ ___
| |\/| / _` \ V / -_) ' \   ~ intelligent projects ~
|_|  |_\__,_|\_/\___|_||_|   v. 1.0.2

build:start:

java:prepare-filesystem:
    [mkdir] Created dir: C:\dev\mavenbook\code\weather\target\classes
Invoking Axis plugin

java:compile:
axis:prepare-filesystem:
    [mkdir] Created dir: C:\dev\mavenbook\code\weather\target\axis\src
    [mkdir] Created dir: C:\dev\mavenbook\code\weather\target\axis\build
    [mkdir] Created dir: C:\dev\mavenbook\code\weather\target\axis\test

test:prepare-filesystem:
    [mkdir] Created dir: C:\dev\mavenbook\code\weather\target\test-classes
    [mkdir] Created dir: C:\dev\mavenbook\code\weather\target\test-reports
find all .wsdl files in directory c:\dev\mavenbook\code\weather/src/wsdl
generate .java files from C:\dev\mavenbook\code\weather\src\wsdl\weather.wsdl

test:test-resources:

java:jar-resources:

axis:axis:
    [axis-wsdl2java] WSDL2Java C:\dev\mavenbook\code\weather\src\wsdl\
weather.wsdl
Parsing XML file:  C:\dev\mavenbook\code\weather\src\wsdl\weather.wsdl
Generating C:\...\gov\weather\forecasts\xml\DWMLgen\schema\ndfdXML_xsd\
FormatType.java
Generating C:\...\gov\weather\forecasts\xml\DWMLgen\schema\ndfdXML_xsd\
ProductType.java
Generating C:\...\gov\weather\forecasts\xml\DWMLgen\schema\ndfdXML_xsd\
WeatherParametersType.java
Generating C:\...\gov\weather\forecasts\xml\DWMLgen\wsdl\ndfdXML_wsdl\
NdfdXMLPortType.java
Generating C:\...\gov\weather\forecasts\xml\DWMLgen\wsdl\ndfdXML_wsdl\
NdfdXMLBindingStub.java
Generating C:\...\gov\weather\forecasts\xml\DWMLgen\wsdl\ndfdXML_wsdl\
NdfdXML.java
Generating C:\...\gov\weather\forecasts\xml\DWMLgen\wsdl\ndfdXML_wsdl\
NdfdXMLLocator.java
Generating C:\...\gov\weather\forecasts\xml\DWMLgen\wsdl\ndfdXML_wsdl\
NdfdXMLTestCase.java
```

```
move the generated testcases to folder c:\dev\mavenbook\code\weather/target/
axis/test
    [move] Moving 1 files to C:\dev\mavenbook\code\weather\target\axis\test

axis:copy:
    [copy] Copying 7 files to C:\dev\mavenbook\code\weather\target\axis\
build
adding c:\dev\mavenbook\code\weather/target/axis/src to the maven.compile.
src.set

axis:compile:
    [echo] Compiling to c:\dev\mavenbook\code\weather/target/classes

java:compile:
    [javac] Compiling 8 source files to C:\dev\mavenbook\code\weather\
target\classes
Note: Some input files use unchecked or unsafe operations.
Note: Recompile with -Xlint:unchecked for details.
BUILD SUCCESSFUL
Total time: 7 seconds
```

When you execute java:compile, Maven will automatically execute
axis:compile, which in turn depends on a number of other goals in the
Axis plug-in which generate source from all WSDL documents contained
in *src/wsdl*. These generated classes will then be automatically added to
the compilation. Since some of the source for this project is generated
from WSDL, it would be redundant to store both the WSDL and the generated source in version control. Inserting axis:compile into the mix with
a preGoal on java:compile includes these classes in the compilation
without requiring you to copy them to *src/main/java*.

The axis:compile goal is misnamed and produces misleading output. While you may think it actually compiles the generated client files, it is simply adding target/axis/src to the compilation source path.

What just happened?

The Axis WSDL2Java tool generates classes in the *target/axis/src* directory. Because you don't plan on modifying the generated classes, you
have defined a preGoal on java:compile which executes axis:compile.
axis:compile adds maven.axis.generated.dir to the maven.compile.
src.set property, which means the generated classes will be compiled
when java:compile is executed. In other words, axis:compile tells
Maven to include *target/axis/src* as a directory which contains source
code to be compiled and packaged in any project artifact.

A postGoal uses the same syntax as a preGoal, and defines a block of Jelly script to be executed before the goal specified in the name attribute.

Okay, so what exactly did this axis:compile goal do again? Here is the
goal definition from this plug-in's *plugin.jelly* file, which you can see in
~/.maven/cache/maven-axis-plugin-0.7/plugin.jelly:

```
<goal name="axis:compile"
    description="Compile the generated .java files."
    prereqs="axis:copy">
```

```
<j:if test="${wsdlPresent == 'true'}">
  <ant:path id="axis.src.set">
    <ant:pathelement location="${maven.axis.build.dir}"/>
  </ant:path>

  <log:info>adding ${maven.axis.generated.dir}
           to the maven.compile.src.set</log:info>
  <maven:addPath id="maven.compile.src.set" refid="axis.src.set"/>
</j:if>
</goal>
```

The operative line has been highlighted: the axis.src.set path is created and subsequently added to maven.compile.src.set. This means the generated Axis classes will now be included in the compile performed by java:compile.

Defining Custom Properties

The Axis plug-in also generates a unit test for your web service, but this generated unit test needs to be customized. For example, the weather SOAP service requires a latitude and longitude to work properly, and the generated unit test uses an invalid value. You need to define a preGoal and postGoal on the axis:wsdl2java goal which copies the unit test to your *src/test/java* directory and excludes it from axis:compile. Because you don't want to overwrite your unit tests every time you run axis:wsdl2java, you need to define a custom property, generate.tests.

How do I do that?

Define a generate.tests property in your *project.properties* file which you will reference in your preGoal and postGoal. Add the following to *project.properties*:

```
# Custom properties
generate.tests = false
```

Now modify your preGoal and postGoal in *maven.xml* to use this new variable to overwrite unit tests only if generate.tests is set to true:

```
<preGoal name="axis:wsdl2java">
  <j:if test="${context.getVariable('generate.tests') == 'true'}">
    <ant:delete dir="${pom.build.unitTestSourceDirectory}/gov"/>
  </j:if>
</preGoal>

<postGoal name="axis:wsdl2java">
  <maven:get var="axis.test" plugin="maven-axis-plugin"
      property="maven.axis.test.dir"/>

  <j:if test="${context.getVariable('generate.tests') == 'true'}">
    <ant:copy todir="${pom.build.unitTestSourceDirectory}">
```

```
        <fileset dir="${ axis.test }"/>
      </ant:copy>
    </j:if>
    <ant:delete dir="${maven.axis.test.dir}/gov"/>
  </postGoal>
```

When you execute maven axis:wsdl2java, Maven will read the properties from *project.properties* and will use the default value of false for the
generate.tests variable, which is set to false. By default, the axis:
wsdl2java goal does not alter the unit tests in ${pom.build.
unitTestSource}. To replace your unit tests with the generated test, execute maven axis:wsdl2java -Dgenerate.tests=true. This should generate the following output for the axis:wsdl2java goal:

```
axis:wsdl2java:
    [copy] Copying 1 file to C:\dev\mavenbook\code\weather\src\test
    [delete] Deleting directory C:\dev\mavenbook\code\weather\target\axis\
test\gov
```

What just happened?

What you are doing here is passive code generation (one-off generation). While you don't need to modify the source code generated from the
WSDL document, you do need to customize the unit test to set an appropriate latitude and longitude. When you need to generate this unit test,
you set the generate.tests property to true. The preGoal on axis:
wsdl2java deletes your unit tests from *src/test* only if the generate.tests
property is set to true, and you should also notice that the end of the
postGoal on axis:wsdl2java always deletes the generated unit tests.

In this lab you defined a variable in *project.properties*. The variable—
generate.tests—provides default behavior, that you can override by
specifying a variable value on the command line. When you ran maven
axis:wsdl2java -Dgenerate.tests=true, you specified a value of
generate.tests which takes precedence over the value defined in
*project.properties.*You also used j:if to test the value of the generate.
tests variable in *maven.xml*:

```
<j:if test="${context.getVariable('generate.tests') == 'true'}">
  <ant:echo>Generate Tests is True</ant:echo>
</j:if>
```

In this example, you are accessing the generate.tests variable by calling the context.getVariable( ) function. The context variable is of type
JellyContext, and it provides access to the variables made available to a
Maven project. The generate.tests variable is compared to a string lit-
eral true. If generate.tests matches true, the ant:echo tag is evaluated.

Maven 2 does away with both the maven.xml and the project. properties files. In Maven 2 all behavior will be customized through the Project Object Model (POM), which will be stored in pom.xml.

If generate.tests is set to true, you might think that the following code fragment would evaluate the reference to ${generate.tests} to true, and would evaluate the ant:echo tag:

```
<j:if test="${generate.tests}">
  <ant:echo>Generate Tests is True</ant:echo>
</j:if>
```

If you write this Jelly script, the ant:echo tag will execute, but it won't execute for the reason you think. The shorthand notation, ${generate.tests}, evaluates to true if a property named generate.tests is available on the Jelly context and that variable is not null. The "." in a Jelly expression can be interpreted in one of two ways. If there is a variable on the Jelly context which matches the name generate.tests, it will be returned. If there is no matching variable, Jelly will consider the "." to signify a method call on a property; ${generate.tests} will evaluate to ${generate.getTests()}, which returns null, as the generated object does not exist. So, ant:echo would execute even if generate.tests was set to the string false, because ${generate.tests} evaluates to true if the content of the variable is nonnull. For this reason, you should always reference a variable using the context.getVariable() method.

The generated unit tests will fail unless they are modified, as they reference a latitude and longitude of 0,0. If you ran axis:wsdl2java and inadvertently removed your NdfdXMLTestCase.java test, you will need to restore the original copy from the example source code.

In this lab, you referenced the ${pom} variable. ${pom} allows you to access everything that was defined in the *project.xml* file, and more. When Jelly encounters an expression, it checks to see if there is a matching property name. If there is no matching property in the Jelly context, Jelly will evaluate the expression as a series of calls to property accessor methods. For example, when you reference a property of the pom variable, you are executing a get method; ${pom.build.sourceDirectory} is equivalent to calling ${pom.getBuild().getSourceDirectory()}. Here is another goal which demonstrates some of the other properties you can access through the ${pom} variable:

```
<goal name="pom-example">
  <ant:echo>Project Name: ${pom.name}</ant:echo>
  <ant:echo>Description: ${pom.description}</ant:echo>
  <ant:echo>Source Directory: ${pom.build.sourceDirectory}</ant:echo>
  <ant:echo>
      Unit Test Directory: ${pom.build.unitTestSourceDirectory}
  </ant:echo>
</goal>
```

The previous goal simply prints the name and the description of a project, followed by the source directory and unit test directory as captured by the `org.apache.maven.project.Build` object obtained by calling `getBuild()` on `org.apache.maven.project.Project`. This goal produces the following output:

```
build:start:

pom-example:
    [echo] Project Name: Test Application
    [echo] Description: An example project
    [echo] Source Directory: C:\dev\mavenbook\code\genapp\test-application\
src\java
    [echo] Unit Test Directory: C:\dev\mavenbook\code\genapp\test-
application\src\test
BUILD SUCCESSFUL
Total time: 1 seconds
```

For a list of the properties accessible from the `${pom}` variable, see the `Project` class JavaDoc at *http://maven.apache.org/apidocs/org/apache/ maven/project/Project.html*. For a list of the properties accessible from the `Dependency` and `Build` objects, see the following JavaDocs: *http:// maven.apache.org/apidocs/org/apache/maven/project/Dependency.html* and *http://maven.apache.org/apidocs/org/apache/maven/project/Build.html*.

You also used the `maven:get` tag to retrieve a property from the Axis plug-in. When referencing plug-in properties, you should always use `maven:get` rather than `${maven.axis.test.dir}`. If a plug-in has not been initialized, a reference to `maven.axis.generated.dir` will cause an error. When you reference a plug-in property with `maven:get`, Maven will initialize the referenced plug-in if it has not already been initialized. You can also set a plug-in property with `maven:set`. Here are two examples of using `maven:get` and `maven:set`: the first call to `maven:get` retrieves the `maven.axis.generated.dir` property from the Axis plug-in, and the second call to `maven:set` sets the value of `maven.axis.generated.dir`:

```
<maven:get var="axis.src" plugin="maven-axis-plugin"
    property="maven.axis.generated.dir"/>

<maven:set plugin="maven-axis-plugin" property="maven.axis.generated.dir"
    value="${basedir}/src/axis"/>
```

To use the Maven tag library, the Maven namespace must be mapped to `jelly:maven`. For more information about the Maven Jelly tag library, see *http://maven.apache.org/reference/maven-jelly-tags/tags.html*. For more information about plug-ins, see Chapter 6.

What about...

...these built-in variables, like ${basedir} and ${pom}? Is there a list?

Yes, there is. Table 2-1 lists some frequently used Maven properties which are made available to goals defined in the *maven.xml* file. The previously defined postGoal and preGoal referenced the ${pom.build. sourceDirectory} variable to get to the directory holding Java source, and the ${pom} variable contains the various pieces of information available from the POM. ${basedir} is another common built-in property which resolves to the root directory of a project.

Table 2-1. A selection of Maven's built-in properties

Built-in property	Resolves to...
${basedir}	Root of a given project. The directory which contains *project.xml* and *maven.xml*.
${maven.build.dir}	*${basedir}/target* directory. Destination directory for intermediate files and generated artifacts.
${maven.build.dest}	*${basedir}/classes* directory. Destination directory for class files.
${user.home}	A user's home directory. On Unix, this is usually something like */home/tobrien*, and on Windows this is *C:\ Documents and Settings\tobrien*.
${maven.home.local}	*${user.home}/.maven* directory.
${maven.repo.remote}	The remote repository from which Maven will download artifacts. Defaults to *http://www.ibiblio.org/maven/*. This property is a comma-delimited list of remote repositories. If an artifact isn't found in the first repository listed, it will try the next repository in the list until either the artifact is located or the end of the list is reached.
${maven.repo.local}	*${maven.home.local}/repository* directory.
${context}	This is a built-in variable in all Jelly scripts, and it is of type JellyContext. This object provides access to the variables a Jelly script has access to. For more information about this object, see *http://jakarta.apache.org/ commons/jelly/apidocs*.
${pom}	Exposes an org.apache.maven.project.Project object for the current project. Use this object to access project paths and resolve dependency paths.
All System properties	The System class exposes a set of properties which can also be accessed. Properties such as java.home, os.arch, and file.separator are among the many System properties exposed.

For a more comprehensive list of Maven properties, see Maven's online reference at *http://maven.apache.org/reference/properties.html*. Chapter 6 delves into the details of how a Maven plug-in can access these properties, and properties specific to a Maven plug-in.

Running the Program from a Custom Goal

Now that you've generated the client library, use Maven to execute the mdn.weather.Weather class and obtain the weather report for Chicago, Illinois.

How do I do that?

Define a custom goal in *maven.xml* that uses Ant's `java` task to execute the mdn.weather.Weather class:

```
<goal name="weather:run" prereqs="jar">

  <ant:java classname="mdn.weather.Weather" fork="true">
    <ant:arg value="41.30"/>
    <ant:arg value="-87.51"/>
    <ant:arg value="1"/>
    <ant:classpath>
      <ant:pathelement
          location="${maven.build.dir}/${maven.final.name}.jar"/>
      <ant:pathelement
          location="${pom.getDependencyPath('commons-discovery:commons-discovery')}"/>
      <ant:pathelement
          location="${pom.getDependencyPath('commons-logging:commons-logging')}"/>
      <ant:pathelement location="${pom.getDependencyPath('axis:axis')}"/>
      <ant:pathelement
          location="${pom.getDependencyPath('axis:axis-jaxrpc')}"/>
      <ant:pathelement location="${pom.getDependencyPath('axis:axis-saaj')}"/>
      <ant:pathelement location="${pom.getDependencyPath('axis:axis-wsdl4j')}"/>
    </ant:classpath>
  </ant:java>

</goal>
```

The Weather class takes three arguments—latitude, longitude, and number of forecast days. In this goal, we've specified the coordinates for Chicago and a single day. When we execute the maven weather:run goal we get the response in the form of an XML document containing our forecast:

```
<?xml version='1.0' ?>
<dwml version='1.0'
    xmlns:xsd="http://www.w3.org/2001/XMLSchema"
    xmlns:xsi="http://www.w3.org/2001/XMLSchema-instance">

// <!--snip-->
<data>
  <location>
    <location-key>point1</location-key>
      <point latitude="41.50" longitude="-87.51"/>
  </location>
```

```
      <parameters applicable-location="point1">
        <temperature type='maximum' units="Fahrenheit"
            time-layout="k-p24h-n1-1">
          <name>Daily Maximum Temperature</name>
          <value>53</value>
        </temperature>
        <temperature type='minimum' units="Fahrenheit"
            time-layout="k-p24h-n1-1">
          <name>Daily Minimum Temperature</name>
          <value>34</value>
        </temperature>
        <probability-of-precipitation type='12 hour'
            units="percent" time-layout="k-p12h-n2-2">
          <name>12 Hourly Probability of Precipitation</name>
          <value>30</value>
          <value>8</value>
        </probability-of-precipitation>
      </parameters>
    </data>

  </dwml>
```

Okay, it's going to be 53 degrees, and there's a 30% chance of rain. Well, that's better than last week!

What just happened?

You used Ant's java task to execute Weather, and you supplied three parameters using ant:arg. The classpath was built by calling the getDependencyPath() method on the ${pom} variable. ${pom. getDependencyPath('axis:axis-saaj')} returns the absolute path to the dependency with groupId axis and artifactId axis-saaj. To reference a dependency with this method, it must be present in your *project.xml* dependencies.

weather:run specifies a prerequisite goal (jar) by listing jar in the prereqs attribute of the goal element. If weather:run depends on more than one goal, this attribute would contain a comma-delimited list of goals. Because weather:run depends on the jar goal, every time you run weather:run you will have to wait for the unit tests to complete. To skip unit tests in any build, add -Dmaven.test.skip=true to the command line. The following command line will execute the Weather class without running unit tests:

```
maven weather:run -Dmaven.test.skip=true
```

While using the ant:java task to execute a Java application is an option, there are better ways to run a program than writing a custom goal in a Maven project. In Chapter 6, you'll write a simple plug-in to execute a JAR.

Defining the Default Goal

If you are frequently running the `weather:run` goal from the command line, you may want to specify a default goal for your Maven project. By specifying a default goal, you can run `maven` from the command line without any arguments, and Maven will execute the `weather:run` goal.

How do I do that?

To set the default goal for a project, simply list the goal name in the `default` attribute of the `project` element:

```
<?xml version="1.0" encoding="UTF-8"?>

<project xmlns:j="jelly:core" xmlns:ant="jelly:ant"
    xmlns:maven="jelly:maven" default="weather:run">

    // ...snip...

</project>
```

When you execute Maven without specifying a goal, Maven will execute the `weather:run` goal. That was easy enough!

Overriding Properties

You have seen that specifying a property on the command line overrides a property defined in *project.properties*, and you've seen that plug-in properties are superseded by *project.properties*. Now that you've seen property overrides in action, take a look at how you can use property overriding to customize behavior for a specific project or a specific user.

How do I do that?

In the "Customizing Plug-in Behavior" lab earlier in this chapter, you set the `maven.axis.serverside` variable in your *project.properties* file. Try running the `axis:wsdl2java` goal and setting the `maven.axis.serverside` property to `true`:

```
maven axis:wsdl2java -Dmaven.axis.serverside=true
```

If you run this, you should see Maven generating a number of different classes and some deployment descriptors for an Apache Axis SOAP service. By setting the `maven.axis.serverside` property from the command line, you have just overridden the value specified in *project.properties*. Properties set from the command line take precedence over properties set anywhere else in Maven.

In fact, Maven has a hierarchy of properties files which you can use to customize a build for a specific project or a specific user. Maven reads properties from the following sources, in the order shown:

${basedir}/project.properties
> This file is a sibling to both *maven.xml* and *project.xml*. This file customizes behavior for a particular project.

${basedir}/build.properties
> This file is also a sibling to *maven.xml* and *project.xml*, but this file is used to customize a specific project's build for a specific user. If you need to change the value of a property for your own build environment but you don't want to affect the properties of other users, add a *build.properties* file to ${basedir}. Values defined in this file will override values defined in *project.properties*. *build.properties* should not be checked into source control; this file is for an individual user to tailor the behavior of a specific project.

${user.home}/build.properties
> Your home directory can contain a *build.properties* file which contains user-specific properties to be used on all projects. This is the proper file in which to configure properties for a proxy server or a remote repository. Properties defined in this file are read for every project, and they supersede the values set in the previous two files.

System properties (specified with the -D flag)
> You've seen this a great deal in this chapter. Setting the value of a property on the command line supersedes all other configuration files. This is the final stop for properties.

In Chapter 3 you will see how projects can inherit properties from parent projects, and Figure 3-3 illustrates the multilayered override mechanism introduced in this lab. As you will also see in Chapter 3, when a project extends another project, it also inherits the properties defined in the parent project's *project.properties* and *build.properties* files.

What just happened?

There are different use cases for using different configuration levels. Something like proxy server configuration is specific to your configuration, and it might be something that is universal to Maven projects you are working with. In this case, universal, user-specific configuration should go into a *build.properties* file in your own home directory. In another case, you may have a specific property which only *you* need to set for a specific project; for example, if you are the release manager for a specific project, you may need to set a `maven.username` property. This kind of user- and project-specific property configuration should be stored in *${basedir}/build.properties*. *${basedir}/build.properties* is a file which you maintain on your local machine (it is not added to a project's source code repository), and it is a mechanism for you to modify the behavior of a specific project to suit your needs. Projects used in a corporate environment demand different configuration values than open source projects using Maven. You may find yourself using the same *${basedir}/build. properties* file for a set of related projects, and defining global defaults in your *${user.home}/build.properties* file.

If you need to configure properties for a project and you would like to share these properties with other developers, add such properties to *${basedir}/project.properties*. This file is checked into source control, and is the project-specific mechanism for setting project configuration.

Enumerating Dependencies

Often you will need to access information from the POM in a Jelly script. How about running this weather program without having to list all of the dependencies as `pathelements`?

How do I do that?

The POM is made available to a Jelly script as a variable—${pom}. Here's a goal which uses the core Jelly tag `forEach` and an Apache Ant `pathelement` tag to create the classpath for running the `mdn.weather. Weather` class:

```
<goal name="weather:run" prereqs="jar">

    <ant:java classname="mdn.weather.Weather" fork="true">
      <ant:arg value="41.30"/>
      <ant:arg value="-87.51"/>
      <ant:arg value="1"/>
      <ant:classpath>
        <ant:pathelement location="${maven.build.dir}/${maven.final.name}.jar"/>
        <j:forEach var="lib" items="${pom.artifacts}">
          <ant:pathelement path="${lib.path}"/>
        </j:forEach>
      </ant:classpath>
    </ant:java>

</goal>
```

Running this goal has the same effect as running `weather:run` from the previous section. This method is preferable to the previous one, as you do not need to list the dependencies in two places. Using this approach, a dependency added to *project.xml* will automatically be added to the classpath.

What just happened?

This example used j:forEach—one of the two loop control structures in Jelly. j:forEach or j:while can be used to iterate over Collection, Map, List, or arrays..

Your custom Jelly goal iterated through the dependencies using the `j:forEach` tag. When you referenced `${pom.artifacts}`, you were referencing the `getArtifacts()` method on the POM which is represented by the `org.apache.maven.project.Project` object. `getArtifacts()` returns a list of `org.apache.maven.project.Artifact` objects which contain information from *project.xml* and information about each dependency's artifact. You then assigned each artifact to a variable named `lib` in a `j:forEach` and referenced the absolute path of each dependency using `${lib.path}`. Some information, such as the path to an artifact exposed through `${pom}`, is derived at runtime. For more information about the `Artifact` object, see the JavaDoc at *http://maven.apache.org/apidocs/ org/apache/maven/repository/Artifact.html*.

Customizing Site Look and Feel

Your weather application is complete, but the Maven-generated site has the same look and feel as every other Maven project. Change the look and feel.

How do I do that?

Customize the behavior of the XDoc plug-in. Take a look at the following properties from *project.properties*:

```
maven.xdoc.date = right
maven.xdoc.date.format = MM/dd/yyyy
maven.xdoc.crumb.separator = >
maven.xdoc.developmentProcessUrl = http://www.slashdot.org
maven.xdoc.poweredBy.title = Powered by the Mighty Maven
maven.xdoc.theme.url=./style/custom.css
```

These properties set the location and format of the site date, the breadcrumb separator, the development process URL, and the "Powered by" title. Run `maven site`, and you will see how these properties made subtle changes to the generated site. Changing the development process URL is important if your organization maintains a page dedicated to your development process. If you leave this property unchanged it will point to a page on the *maven.apache.org* web site.

What just happened?

To customize the look and feel, you will need to alter the CSS used by Maven. To get a sense of the styles used in the Maven theme, take a look at the *target/docs/style* directory of your generated Maven site. Here you will find files named *maven-base.css*, *maven-classic.css*, and *maven-theme.css*. You will need to override these styles to customize the look and feel of Maven. The file is stored in *xdocs/style/custom.css*, and is specified by the `maven.xdoc.theme.url` property and referenced in a generated Maven web site.

For a full list of customizable properties in the XDoc plug-in, take a look at the XDoc plug-in's online documentation at *http://maven.apache.org/reference/plugins/xdoc/*. If you want to get a sense of how to customize a Maven-generated web site, the best place to look is at another project which uses Maven. One project which uses Maven to generate its web site is the Maven project itself (surprise!). Figure 2-2 shows a screenshot of the Maven web site.

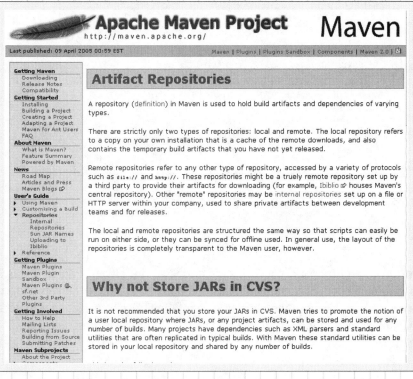

Figure 2-2. Screenshot of a customized Maven web site

The Maven site has customized navigation, external links, date formatting, and PDF generation for the entire site. If you want to customize your site, you should take a look at the *xdocs* directory in the Apache Subversion repository (*http://cvs.apache.org/viewcvs.cgi/maven/maven-1/core/trunk/xdocs/?root=Apache-SVN*). Apache has configured ViewCVS to point to the repository which holds the Maven 1 web site project, and you can use this tool to gain insight into how to customize your build. For example, if you take a look at the *navigation.xml* document in the */maven/maven-1/core/trunk/xdocs* directory, you will see that the following XML fragment defines a collapsible menu item, as shown in the User's Guide section of the navigation in Figure 2-2:

```xml
<menu name="User's Guide">
  <item name="Using Maven" collapse="true" href="/using/index.html">
    <item name="Building JARs" href="/using/jar.html" />
    <item name="Resources" href="/using/resources.html" />
    <item name="Unit Testing" href="/using/tests.html" />
  </item>
  <item name="Customizing a Build" collapse="true"
      href="/using/customising.html">
    <item name="Scripting" href="/reference/scripting.html" />
    <item name="Writing a Plugin" href="/using/developing-plugins.html" />
    <item name="Sharing Plugins" href="/reference/sharing-plugins.html" />
  </item>
  <item name="Repositories" collapse="true"
      href="/using/repositories.html">
    <item name="Internal Repositories"
        href="/reference/internal-repositories.html" />
    <item name="Sun JAR Names"
        href="/reference/standard-sun-jar-names.html" />
    <item name="Uploading to Ibiblio"
        href="/reference/repository-upload.html" />
  </item>
  <item name="Reference" collapse="true" href="/reference/index.html">
    <item name="Glossary" href="/reference/glossary.html" />
    <item name="Conventions" href="/reference/conventions.html" />
    <item name="Project Descriptor" href="/reference/project-descriptor.html" />
  </item>
</item>
</menu>
```

In the same directory, you can take a look at the Maven FAQ in *faq.fml*, and other XDoc documents which are used to create a Maven project web site with comprehensive documentation. Use the Maven project's document as a guide for your own commercial or open source project.

Using the FAQ Plug-in

Many projects contain pages full of frequently asked questions, which provide insight to everything from the reason why a particular project was started to how one can fix common technical problems. The Maven FAQ plug-in is a useful tool for creating such a page.

How do I do that?

To use the FAQ plug-in, list the plug-in in your *project.xml* reports element as follows:

```
<reports>
  <report>maven-faq-plugin</report>
</reports>
```

Now that you have the report activated, create the *xdocs/faq.fml* file with the following content:

```
<?xml version="1.0" encoding="UTF-8"?>
<faqs title="Frequently Asked Questions">

    <part id="general">
      <title>General</title>

      <faq id="whats-weather">
        <question>
          What is the Weather project?
        </question>
        <answer>
          <p>
            The Weather project is an example from the Maven
            Developer's Notebook.  It is an attempt to demonstrate
            simple Maven customization techniques with a project
            that isn't going to bore the reader to death.
          </p>
        </answer>
      </faq>

      <faq id="why-axis">
        <question>
          Why did you choose the Axis plug-in?
        </question>
        <answer>
          <p>
            The Axis plug-in was selected because it happens to
            be a useful and complex tool that is easy to introduce.
          </p>
        </answer>
      </faq>
    </part>
```

The reports element is not additive. If you specify only one report in this element, only one report is generated. You'll need to list all the reports you want explicitly in the reports element.

```
<part id="install">
  <title>Installation</title>

  <faq id="how-install">
    <question>
      How do I install Weather?
    </question>
    <answer>
      <p>Simple, check it out of Subversion, and run maven wsdl2java.</p>
    </answer>
  </faq>
</part>
</faqs>
```

Now, generate the site with maven site, and load *target/docs/index.html* in a browser. If you click Project Reports and FAQs, you should see the page shown in Figure 2-3.

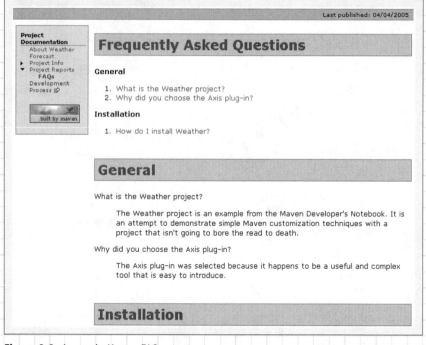

Figure 2-3. A sample Maven FAQ report

What just happened?

You activated the FAQ plug-in by listing it in *project.xml*'s reports element. Then you wrote an XML document containing a series of frequently asked questions. When you generated the site, this FAQ was transformed into a web page, and linked from the Project Reports submenu.

Multiproject Maven

In Chapter 1 you saw how you can create and build a simple project with a single class. In real life, projects are always more complex, and your projects may need to generate several artifacts (JARs, WARs, EARs, Web Start applications, etc.). Along with multiple artifacts, you will need to perform different build operations for different types of artifacts; for example, EAR files must be packaged for J2EE applications, some projects may include automated functional tests, applications may need to be deployed to an application server, or a project may need to execute a Web Start application. This list could go on forever, and it seems that the longer a project exists, the more complex build requirements become. In Maven, you manage build entropy by splitting a single monolithic monster project into smaller, more manageable subprojects.

Dividing and Conquering

When developing object-oriented code, it is good practice to implement a separation-of-concerns strategy. In a complex software engineering effort, you manage complexity by organizing logic into components which are tightly focused (or concerned) with a specific part of a project or process. You can apply this same idea to a project's build. If you have a huge, multi-artifact project, having a big build with everything stuffed in is asking for maintenance hell. Fortunately, Maven is here to help us break down our project into subprojects.

How do I do that?

Let's take a web application example. Imagine a simple web application with a Servlet container showing the Quote of the Day (QOTD). Your first goal is to identify the different Maven subprojects you need to create to break such an application into distinct subprojects. The QOTD application uses Rome, a Really Simple Syndication (RSS) and Atom Utilities library, to parse a publicly available quote-of-the-day feed at *http:// www.quotationspage.com/data/qotd.rss*.

Figure 3-1 illustrates the QOTD web application that has been separated into four interdependent modules. Each circle represents a separate Maven subproject which creates an artifact. Each arrow represents a dependency: the packager project depends on the web project, and the web project depends on the core project.

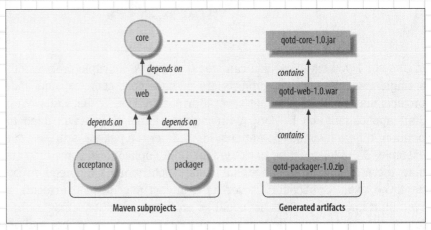

Figure 3-1. Maven subprojects for the QOTD web application

Break it up! Large projects are difficult to maintain. Do not hesitate to refactor your project into multiple subprojects.

Here's a rundown of what each subproject contains:

core

The core subproject contains business logic for obtaining the quote of the day. Such logic is independent of any specific presentation layer, and core generates a JAR artifact named *qotd-core-1.0.jar*.

web

The web subproject contains all the classes for the QOTD web application. In this case, the web subproject is composed of servlets, JSP files, and HTML files. These classes depend on business logic from the core artifact to obtain quotes. The web subproject generates a WAR artifact named *qotd-web-1.0.war*.

acceptance

The acceptance subproject executes acceptance tests on the web application using *HtmlUnit* (*http://htmlunit.sourceforge.net*), which is a framework that extends JUnit to test web pages. To start your web application, you are going to use the Jetty plug-in, which uses the

Chapter 3: Multiproject Maven

Jetty (*http://jetty.mortbay.org*) Servlet container. Thus, the acceptance subproject requires that both the core and web subprojects be built before its tests can be executed. Note that the acceptance subproject does not generate an artifact.

packager

> packager generates a zip file containing the distribution of the web application project. The zip file contains the web application in a WAR file, and a *README* with installation instructions. In a real web application project, you could package a container so that the web application is a standalone application that can be executed as is by its users.

What about...

...having a single project with a single source directory? Why couldn't I just put the business logic and the packaging goals in the web project?

You would soon find out that this is not possible with Maven if you wish to benefit from the existing plug-ins to the full extent. In Maven, the following rule applies: one build project must generate only one primary artifact (JAR, WAR, EAR, etc.)—one project, one artifact. All the existing Maven plug-ins are built following this rule. Maven projects can generate multiple secondary artifacts such as JavaDoc files, sources packaged as zip files, and reports, but a single project can generate only a single primary artifact.

For example, the Java plug-in supports only a single source directory, so you wouldn't be able to elegantly use it for compiling sources located in different directories. The same applies for the Test plug-in, which can only execute unit tests located in a single source directory. Maven was designed with multiproject builds in mind, and for this reason you will find it impossible to create a monster "frankenproject" with a large, distributed source path.

Using POM Inheritance

Maven projects are completely described by a Project Object Model (POM), and when you break a project into subprojects, each subproject will have its own POM. Because a series of related projects most likely originated from the same organization, have the same developer team, and use a similar set of dependencies, related project POMs will tend to contain duplicate data. From the previous example, core would contain the same developers element as web, which would contain the same developers element as the `packager` project. Configuration duplication is just as bad as code duplication, and to reduce the amount of work to maintain related POMs you'll need to have each POM inherit from a super-POM. When a project's POM inherits from a common POM, subprojects need to specify only how they're different from the main project. Maven supports project inheritance, which means that any subproject can inherit from its parent's *project.xml*, *maven.xml*, and properties files (*project.properties* and *build.properties*).

How do I do that?

Figure 3-2 shows the four subprojects' *project.xml* files, along with a new *common/* directory that you have created. The *common/* directory contains the shared *project.xml* and *project.properties* files you want all subprojects to inherit from. You can put in the *common/* directory any Maven build-related file you wish to share between your Maven subprojects; this includes *project.properties*, *project.xml*, and *maven.xml*.

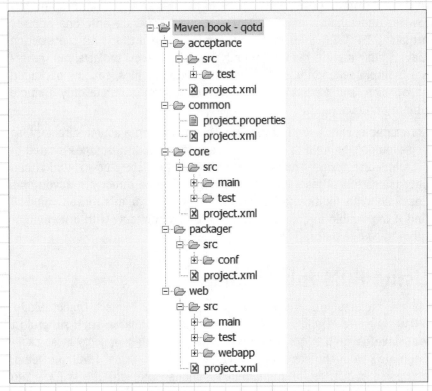

Figure 3-2. Maven build files inheriting from common definitions

Take a look at the *common/project.xml* file:

```xml
<?xml version="1.0"?>
<project>
  <pomVersion>3</pomVersion>
  <groupId>mdn</groupId>
  <currentVersion>1.0</currentVersion>
  <organization>
    <name>O'Reilly</name>
    <url>http://www.oreilly.com/</url>
    <logo>http://www.oreilly.com/images/oreilly/oreilly_header1.gif</logo>
  </organization>
  <inceptionYear>2005</inceptionYear>

  <url>
    http://www.mavenbook.org/projects/${pom.groupId}/${pom.artifactId}
  </url>

  <siteAddress>www.mavenbook.org</siteAddress>
  <siteDirectory>
    /var/www/html/mavenbook/projects/${pom.groupId}/${pom.artifactId}
  </siteDirectory>

  <mailingLists/>

  <developers>
    [...]
  </developers>

</project>
```

All those XML tags are going to be common for all other subprojects.
Every project is going to have the same organization, the same inception
year, and the same URL format. The project's URL is constructed using
references to the ${pom} variable, as introduced in Chapter 2. When
Maven evaluates the url or the siteDirectory for a subproject, it will
use the POM values specific to that subproject. To see how a project
would inherit the values defined in *common/project.xml*, take a look at
core/project.xml:

```xml
<?xml version="1.0"?>
<project>
  <extend>../common/project.xml</extend>
  <name>QOTD Core</name>
  <artifactId>qotd-core</artifactId>
  <package>mdn.qotd.core</package>
  <shortDescription>QOTD core library</shortDescription>
  <description>
    QOTD core library
  </description>

  <dependencies>
    <dependency>
      <groupId>rome</groupId>
```

You achieve inheritance by using the extend element in a project's project.xml file.

Most elements in the parent POM are overridden by the child's POM elements. However, the dependencies elements are additive (i.e., these elements will be aggregated).

```
            <artifactId>rome</artifactId>
            <version>0.5</version>
        </dependency>
        <dependency>
            <groupId>jdom</groupId>
            <artifactId>jdom</artifactId>
            <version>1.0</version>
        </dependency>
    </dependencies>

    <build>
        <sourceDirectory>src/main</sourceDirectory>
        <unitTestSourceDirectory>src/test</unitTestSourceDirectory>
        <unitTest>
            <includes>
                <include>**/*Test.java</include>
            </includes>
        </unitTest>
    </build>

</project>
```

The important item is the extend element, which specifies a parent POM
to inherit from.

TIP

Prior to Maven 1.0.2, you had to use the ${basedir} property to
prefix directories defined in the POM (such as for the extend tag, or
for the sourceDirectory tag). Otherwise, the project would not
build correctly when using the Multiproject plug-in. This is not necessary anymore.

What just happened?

You created a common configuration for a series of subprojects. You
extracted common information to the *common/project.xml* file, and you
did this by using the extend element.

TIP

In Maven 2 it will be possible to define build elements to be inher-
ited by subprojects in a special section in the POMs of the parent
projects. Thus, you will not need to have a *common/* directory, as
you do for Maven 1.

This extend element tells Maven to inherit not only from a parent's
project.xml, but also from the parent's *maven.xml* and *project.properties*

files. Actually you can't decide what you inherit: it's everything or nothing. If the *common/maven.xml* file defines a custom goal, it will be available to the subproject, and if *common/project.properties* defines a set of properties, they will also be available to a subproject. Although not discussed in this book, it is possible to have any number of inheritance levels; a subproject could extend an intermediate *project.xml* which, in turn, could extend another *project.xml*. Each extension brings with it properties from *project.properties* and goals from *maven.xml*.

Note that *common/project.xml* contains the following element with references to ${pom.groupId} and ${pom.artifactId}:

```
<url>http://www.mavenbook.org/projects/${pom.groupId}/${pom.artifactId}</url>
```

The value of the url element is evaluated for each subproject, and in the case of the core project, this value would translate to *http://www.mavenbook.org/projects/mdn/qotd-core*. The *common/project.xml* file defines the value for the groupId, and each subproject's id element is used as the artifactId. In this example, you have configured a single *project.xml* which sets the structure of each subproject's URL. Each subproject will have a different URL because variable substitution is performed for each specific subproject.

References to variables in the common project.xml file are evaluated in the context of each subproject. ${pom} referenced in common/project.xml is replaced with the POM object of each subproject.

As mentioned previously, this example uses an RSS and Atom parsing framework known as Rome, and the core project defines two dependencies in *core/project.xml*: the Rome library and JDOM.

What about...

...the precedence level between properties defined in your user home, on the command line, in your parent projects (there can be several inheritance levels), and in your project?

This is something important to keep in mind. The properties are resolved in the following order (the last property set takes precedence over the previous ones), as shown in Figure 3-3:

- *[parent]/project.properties*
- *[parent]/build.properties*
- *[project]/project.properties*
- *[project]/build.properties*
- *[userhome]/build.properties*
- System properties

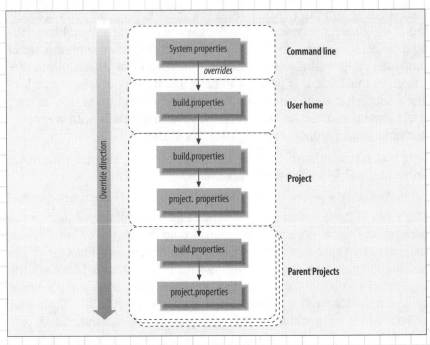

Figure 3-3. Level of precedence for Maven properties

Writing the Quote Generator

Before you go any further with the multiproject setup, let's take a look at how the core project has implemented the quote generator. This application uses the online quote generator located at *http://www. quotationspage.com/*; a site which generates an RSS feed of quotes. To parse this feed, you will make use of the Rome framework feed parser (*https://rome.dev.java.net/*) which has built-in support for parsing RSS and Atom feeds. To get started, add the following code to *core/src/main/ mdn/qotd/core/QuoteGenerator.java*:

```
package mdn.qotd.core;

import java.net.URL;

import com.sun.syndication.feed.synd.SyndContent;
import com.sun.syndication.feed.synd.SyndEntry;
import com.sun.syndication.feed.synd.SyndFeed;
import com.sun.syndication.io.SyndFeedInput;
import com.sun.syndication.io.XmlReader;

public class QuoteGenerator
{
    private static final String QUOTE_URL =
        "http://www.quotationspage.com/data/qotd.rss";
```

```java
    public String generate()
    {
        SyndFeed quoteFeed;
        try
        {
            SyndFeedInput input = new SyndFeedInput();
            quoteFeed = input.build(new XmlReader(new URL(QUOTE_URL)));
        }
        catch (Exception e)
        {
            throw new RuntimeException("Failed to get RSS Quote Feed ["
                + QUOTE_URL + "]", e);
        }

        SyndEntry firstQuoteEntry =
            (SyndEntry) quoteFeed.getEntries().get(0);
        SyndContent firstQuoteContent =
            (SyndContent) firstQuoteEntry.getContents().get(0);

        return firstQuoteContent.getValue();
    }

}
```

If you are test-infected, you are probably wondering why you didn't write a unit test for QuoteGenerator before writing our parsing logic. To make up for this oversight, write a quick test for the QuoteGenerator class in *core/src/test/mdn/qotd/core/QuoteGeneratorTest.java*:

```java
package mdn.qotd.core;

import mdn.qotd.core.QuoteGenerator;
import junit.framework.TestCase;

public class QuoteGeneratorTest extends TestCase
{
    public void testGenerate()
    {
        assertTrue(new QuoteGenerator().generate().length() > 0);
    }
}
```

The quote RSS feed sends a different quote every day, and because of this, it is impossible to perform an assertEquals() on the generated quote string. This test simply tests to see that a quote has been returned from *quotationspage.com* and that it has been successfully parsed without throwing a RuntimeException.

What just happened?

Introducing Rome is beyond the scope of this Notebook, but you should know that Rome is an innovative and useful utility that makes RSS and

Atom feeds easier to manage. You've created a program to parse an RSS feed from *quotationspage.com*, and you are returning the first quote from this feed. The web subproject is going to call the generate( ) method on QuoteGenerator to generate a quote for display on a web page.

Sharing Artifacts Through the Local Maven Repository

Figure 3-1 illustrates the dependencies between the subproject, and from this diagram, you can see that the web subproject depends upon the core subproject. How do you share artifacts between projects in Maven?

How do I do that?

You do this through the local Maven repository, which was introduced in Chapter 1. The core build will publish its JAR to the repository and the web build will define a dependency on the core JAR.

To refresh your memory, your local repository resides in *~/.maven/repository* on Unix, or *%USERPROFILE%\.maven\repository* on Windows. Publishing a JAR to your local repository is as simple as executing the jar:install goal:

```
C:\dev\mavenbook\code\qotd\core>maven jar:install

 __ __
|  \/  |__ _Apache__ ___
| |\/| / _` \ V / -_) ' \   ~ intelligent projects ~
|_|  |_\__,_|\_/\___|_||_|   v. 1.0.2

build:start:

java:prepare-filesystem:
    [mkdir] Created dir: C:\dev\mavenbook\code\qotd\core\target\classes

java:compile:
    [echo] Compiling to C:\dev\mavenbook\code\qotd\core/target/classes
    [javac] Compiling 1 source file to C:\dev\mavenbook\code\qotd\core\
target\classes

java:jar-resources:

test:prepare-filesystem:
    [mkdir] Created dir: C:\dev\mavenbook\code\qotd\core\target\test-classes
    [mkdir] Created dir: C:\dev\mavenbook\code\qotd\core\target\test-reports

test:test-resources:

test:compile:
```

```
    [javac] Compiling 1 source file to C:\dev\mavenbook\code\qotd\core\
target\test-classes

test:test:
    [junit] Testsuite: mdn.qotd.core.QuoteGeneratorTest
    [junit] Tests run: 1, Failures: 0, Errors: 0, Time elapsed: 4,226 sec
    [junit]
    [junit] Testcase: testGenerate took 3,926 sec

jar:jar:
    [jar] Building jar: C:\dev\mavenbook\code\qotd\core\target\qotd-core-1.
0.jar
Copying: from 'C:\dev\mavenbook\code\qotd\core\target\qotd-core-1.0.jar' to:
'C:\Documents and Settings\Vincent Massol\.maven\repository\mdn\jars\qotd-
core-1.0.jar'
Copying: from 'C:\dev\mavenbook\code\qotd\core\project.xml' to: 'C:\
Documents and Settings\Vincent Massol\.maven\repository\mdn\poms\qotd-core-
1.0.pom'
BUILD SUCCESSFUL
Total time: 10 seconds
```

Maven is very fond of unit testing. Every time you try to create a JAR file or deploy a site, Maven will run those unit tests.

The core JAR is now located in *[MAVEN_REPO]/mdn/jars/qotd-core-1.0. jar*. The jar:install depends on the jar:jar goal which, in turn, triggers the java:compile and test:test goals.

Now that *qotd-core-1.0.jar* is installed in your local Maven repository, how do you reference it from another project? To reference the core JAR from another Maven project, add the following dependency in *project.xml*:

```
<dependency>
  <groupId>mdn</groupId>
  <artifactId>qotd-core</artifactId>
  <version>${pom.currentVersion}</version>
</dependency>
```

Note that you are using the expression ${pom.currentVersion}, which refers to the value of the currentVersion element (defined in *common/ project.xml* with a value of 1.0). In this manner you avoid hardcoding it so that you don't need to modify the version element whenever the project's version is modified.

WARNING

The current version of QOTD is defined for all subprojects in *common/project.xml*. Referencing ${pom.currentVersion} in subprojects that do not inherit the same currentVersion element would produce errors. This technique requires all subprojects to be on the same version, which is generally the case for multiprojects. All subprojects should be released together in a multiproject. If some subprojects should be released individually, consider separating them from the multiproject.

What just happened?

Maven enforces the decoupling of projects by sharing artifacts through the local repository. Instead of projects depending on each other directly, each project depends on the contents of the local repository. The web subproject simply depends upon the qotd-core artifact in the local repository. Maven projects do not relate to each other through relative paths or environment variables, as this creates brittle build systems and steep learning curves for new developers. Projects simply depend on artifacts from other projects.

We remember the old times when projects such as Jakarta Taglibs were using Ant, and projects were tightly coupled with one another through the use of relative paths (e.g., *../../otherproject/target/dist/otherproject. jar*). The only way to build Jakarta Taglibs was to check out a few sibling projects, download a few JAR files, and configure a user-specific configuration file—*build.properties-sample*—which was stored in source control. All of this made build maintenance a nightmare, as modifying one project's build had repercussions on other projects. The more complex an Ant build became, and the more interdependent projects became, the more build maintenance came to resemble an endless game of whack-a-mole. No more of this futility with Maven!

Using the WAR Plug-in

Now that you have built the core subproject, you should move on to the web subproject. This is a good occasion for you to learn how to use the Maven WAR plug-in. Figure 3-4 shows the directory structure for the web subproject.

A project that uses the WAR plug-in contains three source trees:

src/main
> Contains the runtime Java sources. There is only one servlet (mdn. qotd.web.QuoteServlet) for the web subproject.

src/test
> Contains the JUnit tests for unit testing the Java code found in *src/ main*. The mdn.qotd.web.QuoteServletTest tests methods from the QuoteServlet servlet. Note that these unit tests are performed in isolation (i.e., without a running container). They are not functional tests.

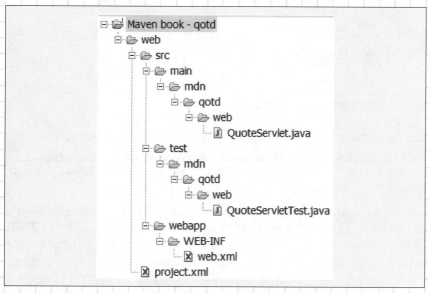

Figure 3-4. Directory structure for the web subproject

src/webapp

Contains all the web application resources (HTML files, JSP files, configuration files, etc.). For the web subproject you have only a *WEB-INF/web.xml* file, which maps the QuoteServlet to a web context. This exceedingly simple *web.xml* file follows:

```xml
<?xml version="1.0" encoding="ISO-8859-1"?>

<!DOCTYPE web-app
    PUBLIC "-//Sun Microsystems, Inc.//DTD Web Application 2.3//EN"
    "http://java.sun.com/dtd/web-app_2_3.dtd">

<web-app>

  <servlet>
    <servlet-name>QuoteServlet</servlet-name>
    <servlet-class>mdn.qotd.web.QuoteServlet</servlet-class>
  </servlet>

  <servlet-mapping>
    <servlet-name>MainServlet</servlet-name>
    <url-pattern>/</url-pattern>
  </servlet-mapping>

</web-app>
```

As shown in Chapter 1, *src/main* and *src/test* locations are defined in the *project.xml* file under the build element. The following build element tells Maven where to find the source and tests for this project:

```
<build>
  <sourceDirectory>src/main</sourceDirectory>
  <unitTestSourceDirectory>src/test</unitTestSourceDirectory>
  <unitTest>
    <includes>
      <include>**/*Test.java</include>
    </includes>
  </unitTest>
</build>
```

The location of the web application resources (*src/webapp*) is not defined in *project.xml*. It is an extension brought by the WAR plug-in. It is configured by a plug-in property named `maven.war.src`, which defaults to the *src/webapp* location.

Remember that the web subproject depends on the core subproject, which means you want to have the core JAR bundled in your WAR, under *WEB-INF/lib*. You also need to bundle the Rome and JDOM JARs which are required by the core subproject. You achieve this by tagging the core, Rome, and JDOM JARs' dependency elements defined in *project. xml* with the `war.bundle` property, as shown here:

```
<dependency>
  <groupId>mdn</groupId>
  <artifactId>qotd-core</artifactId>
  <version>${pom.currentVersion}</version>
  <properties>
    <war.bundle>true</war.bundle>
  </properties>
</dependency>
<dependency>
  <groupId>rome</groupId>
  <artifactId>rome</artifactId>
  <version>0.5</version>
  <properties>
    <war.bundle>true</war.bundle>
  </properties>
</dependency>
<dependency>
  <groupId>jdom</groupId>
  <artifactId>jdom</artifactId>
  <version>1.0</version>
  <properties>
    <war.bundle>true</war.bundle>
  </properties>
</dependency>
```

Tagging a dependency with a property is a common feature used by several Maven plug-ins. It allows you to specify some special actions that the plug-in should perform on certain artifacts. Here, the WAR plug-in will copy the core JAR to *WEB-INF/lib* when asked to generate the WAR by calling the war goal.

Maven copies these dependencies to *WEB-INF/lib* during the war:webapp
goal execution in the following console output:

```
C:\dev\mavenbook\code\qotd\web>maven war

 __ __
|  \/  |__ _Apache__ ___
| |\/| / _` \ V / -) ' \   ~ intelligent projects ~
|_|  |_\__,_|\_/\___|_||_|   v. 1.0.2

build:start:

war:init:

war:war-resources:
    [mkdir] Created dir: C:\dev\mavenbook\code\qotd\web\target\qotd-web
    [mkdir] Created dir: C:\dev\mavenbook\code\qotd\web\target\qotd-web\WEB-
INF
    [copy] Copying 1 file to C:\dev\mavenbook\code\qotd\web\target\qotd-web
    [copy] Copying 1 file to C:\dev\mavenbook\code\qotd\web\target\qotd-web\
WEB-INF

java:prepare-filesystem:
    [mkdir] Created dir: C:\dev\mavenbook\code\qotd\web\target\classes

java:compile:
    [echo] Compiling to C:\dev\mavenbook\code\qotd\web/target/classes
    [javac] Compiling 1 source file to C:\dev\mavenbook\code\qotd\web\
target\classes

java:jar-resources:

test:prepare-filesystem:
    [mkdir] Created dir: C:\dev\mavenbook\code\qotd\web\target\test-classes
    [mkdir] Created dir: C:\dev\mavenbook\code\qotd\web\target\test-reports

test:test-resources:

test:compile:
    [javac] Compiling 1 source file to C:\dev\mavenbook\code\qotd\web\
target\test-classes

test:test:
    [junit] Testsuite: mdn.qotd.web.QuoteServletTest
    [junit] Tests run: 1, Failures: 0, Errors: 0, Time elapsed: 0,261 sec
    [junit]
    [junit] Testcase: testSendQuote took 0,011 sec
```

```
war:webapp:
    [echo] Assembling webapp qotd-web
    [mkdir] Created dir: C:\dev\mavenbook\code\qotd\web\target\qotd-web\WEB-
INF\lib
    [mkdir] Created dir: C:\dev\mavenbook\code\qotd\web\target\qotd-web\WEB-
INF\tld
    [mkdir] Created dir: C:\dev\mavenbook\code\qotd\web\target\qotd-web\WEB-
INF\classes
    [copy] Copying 1 file to C:\dev\mavenbook\code\qotd\web\target\qotd-web\
WEB-INF\lib
    [copy] Copying 1 file to C:\dev\mavenbook\code\qotd\web\target\qotd-web\
WEB-INF\lib
    [copy] Copying 1 file to C:\dev\mavenbook\code\qotd\web\target\qotd-web\
WEB-INF\lib
    [copy] Copying 1 file to C:\dev\mavenbook\code\qotd\web\target\qotd-web\
WEB-INF\classes

war:war:
    [echo] Building WAR qotd-web
    [jar] Building jar: C:\dev\mavenbook\code\qotd\web\target\qotd-web.war
BUILD SUCCESSFUL
Total time: 3 seconds
```

As shown in Figure 3-5, the generated WAR—*target/qotd-web.war*—contains the core, Rome, and JDOM JARs in *WEB-INF/lib*.

Name	Type	Modified	Size	Ratio	Packed	Path ▲
Manifest.mf	MF File	25/03/2005 22:08	344	46%	186	meta-inf\
web.xml	XML Document	25/03/2005 22:08	474	46%	256	web-inf\
QuoteServlet.class	CLASS File	25/03/2005 22:08	1 299	49%	660	WEB-INF\classes\mdn\qotd\web\
jdom-1.0.jar	Executable Jar File	25/03/2005 22:08	153 253	6%	144 824	WEB-INF\lib\
qotd-core-1.0.jar	Executable Jar File	25/03/2005 22:08	1 716	23%	1 321	WEB-INF\lib\
rome-0.5.jar	Executable Jar File	25/03/2005 22:08	156 711	10%	141 184	WEB-INF\lib\

Figure 3-5. Content of generated WAR file showing that the core JAR has been included

Finally, you need to deploy the web WAR to the Maven local repository so that it can be made available for the acceptance and packager subprojects (see Figure 3-1). You achieve this by calling the war:install goal from the WAR plug-in:

```
C:\dev\mavenbook\code\qotd\web>maven war:install
[...]
war:war:
    [echo] Building WAR qotd-web
    [jar] Building jar: C:\dev\mavenbook\code\qotd\web\target\qotd-web.war
Copying: from 'C:\dev\mavenbook\code\qotd\web\target\qotd-web.war' to: 'C:\
Documents and Settings\Vincent Massol\.maven\repository\mdn\wars\qotd-web-1.
0.war'
Copying: from 'C:\dev\mavenbook\code\qotd\web\project.xml' to: 'C:\Documents
and Settings\Vincent Massol\.maven\repository\mdn\poms\qotd-web-1.0.pom'
BUILD SUCCESSFUL
Total time: 3 seconds
```

What just happened?

You just created a WAR file by running `maven war`. You then installed a WAR into your local repository using `maven war:install`. To bundle dependencies with the generated WAR file, you set the `war.bundle` property on each dependency to `true`.

Your local repository holds more than JARs. It can also hold WAR files, or any artifact created by Maven.

What about...

...the other build actions available from the WAR plug-in?

You can obtain the full list of goals by typing `maven -P war`. You can find more information about the goals and properties of this plug-in at *http://maven.apache.org/reference/plugins/war/goals.html* and *http://maven.apache.org/reference/plugins/war/properties.html*. Others not discussed in this section include support for adding tag libraries, generating expanded WARs (useful for quick round-trip development for `Servlet` containers supporting dynamic reloading), and installing the generated WAR in the Maven remote repository.

Using the Jetty Plug-in to Start a Web Application

Functional testing is usually harder than unit testing because functional testing requires a complete execution environment. This requirement is particularly tough to satisfy when you are testing a web application, as you need to start your application in a `Servlet` container. This lab demonstrates how to use the Jetty plug-in to start the web application from Figure 3-1, in the Jetty `Servlet` container. We selected Jetty because it is a very fast container and a quality Jetty plug-in is available for Maven.

Jetty takes only a few milliseconds to start up.

How do I do that?

As shown in Figure 3-1, there is an `acceptance` subproject from which you will execute your acceptance tests (otherwise know as functional tests).

The `web` project that you used earlier generated the WAR that you wish to test functionally. You need to tell the Jetty plug-in to deploy this WAR. You do this by defining a dependency in the `acceptance` project's *project.xml*, and by tagging the dependency with the `jetty.bundle` property:

```
<dependency>
  <groupId>mdn</groupId>
```

```
      <artifactId>qotd-web</artifactId>
      <version>${pom.currentVersion}</version>
      <properties>
        <jetty.bundle>true</jetty.bundle>
      </properties>
      <type>war</type>
    </dependency>
```

Let's configure the Jetty plug-in so that Jetty runs on port 8081 (by default it runs on 8080). You achieve this by adding the following property in the *project.properties* file, in the *acceptance/* directory:

```
maven.jetty.port = 8081
```

Start Jetty by executing the `jetty:run` goal as follows:

```
C:\dev\mavenbook\code\qotd\acceptance>maven jetty:run

  __  __
 |  \/  |___ _Apache__ ___
 | |\/| / _` \ V / -_)  ' \   ~ intelligent projects ~
 |_|  |_\__,_|\_/\___|_||_|  v. 1.0.2

build:start:

jetty:prepare-filesystem:

jetty:config:

jetty:run:
    [java] 09:17:54.414 EVENT  Checking Resource aliases
    [java] 09:17:54.714 EVENT  Starting Jetty/4.2.17
    [java] 09:17:54.764 WARN!! Delete existing temp dir C:\DOCUME~1\[...][/
qotd-web,jar:file:/C:/Documents%20and%20Settings/[...]/.maven/repository/
mdn/wars/qotd-web-1.0.war!/]
    [java] 09:17:54.884 EVENT  Started WebApplicationContext[/qotd-web,jar:
file:/C:/Documents%20and%20Settings/[...]/.maven/repository/mdn/wars/qotd-
web-1.0.war!/]
    [java] 09:17:54.924 EVENT  jsp: init
    [java] 09:17:55.135 EVENT  default: init
    [java] 09:17:55.135 EVENT  invoker: init
    [java] 09:17:55.215 EVENT  Started SocketListener on 0.0.0.0:8081
    [java] 09:17:55.215 EVENT  Started org.mortbay.jetty.Server@117a8bd
```

There; you've used Maven to start a Servlet container, and your web application is now running. You can open a browser and go to *http://localhost:8081/qotd-web/* to get the output of the QuoteServlet (see Figure 3-6).

To stop the running container, simply press Ctrl-C in the Maven Console window.

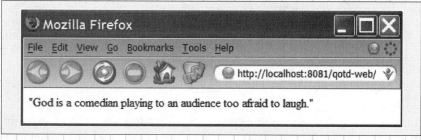

Figure 3-6. Output from QuoteServlet from the web subproject

What just happened?

You just started Jetty, a `Servlet` container, and all you had to do was add a simple property to the dependency on `qotd-web`. Take note of the level of convenience Maven provides to your development cycle. Instead of starting your own `Servlet` container and copying a WAR file to some deployment directory, you simply ran `maven jetty:run` and a `Servlet` container started to execute your project.

Executing HtmlUnit Tests

Great, you've started a `Servlet` container! Now you will learn how to use this container to execute functional tests to validate the web subproject's WAR.

How do I do that?

First things first; write an HtmlUnit test. The purpose of this chapter is not to teach you the intricacies of HtmlUnit (see *http://htmlunit. sourceforge.net/* for a good tutorial). Instead, this lab will focus on how you can integrate HtmlUnit with Maven and the Jetty plug-in. Without further ado, here's what a test of the `QuoteServlet` could look like:

```
package mdn.qotd.acceptance;

import java.net.URL;

import com.gargoylesoftware.htmlunit.WebClient;
import com.gargoylesoftware.htmlunit.html.HtmlPage;

import junit.framework.TestCase;

public class QuoteServletTest extends TestCase
{
    public void testMainServletPage() throws Exception
    {
```

```
                    WebClient webClient = new WebClient();
                    URL url = new URL("http://localhost:8081/qotd-web");
                    HtmlPage page = (HtmlPage) webClient.getPage(url);
                    String content = page.getWebResponse().getContentAsString();
                    assertTrue(content.startsWith("\""));
                    assertTrue(content.endsWith("\""));
            }
        }
```

You will notice that an HtmlUnit test case is a JUnit test case (it extends JUnit's TestCase class), and this means that you can use the Maven Test plug-in to execute it. Before doing so you need to add all of HtmlUnit's JAR dependencies to the acceptance subproject's *project.xml*:

```
<dependency>
    <groupId>htmlunit</groupId>
    <artifactId>htmlunit</artifactId>
    <version>1.3</version>
</dependency>
<dependency>
    <groupId>nekohtml</groupId>
    <artifactId>nekohtml</artifactId>
    <version>0.9.4</version>
</dependency>
<dependency>
    <groupId>commons-httpclient</groupId>
    <artifactId>commons-httpclient</artifactId>
    <version>2.0.2</version>
</dependency>
<dependency>
    <groupId>commons-logging</groupId>
    <artifactId>commons-logging</artifactId>
    <version>1.0.4</version>
</dependency>
```

TIP

What a pain it is to enter all those HtmlUnit dependencies! You should really have to enter only one HtmlUnit dependency and Maven should figure out how to include HtmlUnit's own dependencies. Good news! You can, with a feature called Transitive Dependencies, which is being implemented in Maven 2.

Executing the test:test goal now would fail, because you also need to have a container started. The solution is to start the container in one thread using the Jetty plug-in and to start the Test plug-in in another thread. You can achieve this by writing some custom Jelly code in the *acceptance/maven.xml* file and using the j:thread element of the core Jelly tag library:

```xml
<?xml version="1.0"?>

<project default="test:test"
    xmlns:j="jelly:core"
    xmlns:ant="jelly:ant">

  <preGoal name="test:test">
    <j:thread>
      <attainGoal name="jetty:run"/>
    </j:thread>
    <ant:waitfor>
      <ant:http url="http://localhost:${maven.jetty.port}/qotd-web"/>
    </ant:waitfor>
  </preGoal>

</project>
```

Notice that you are using a preGoal, which means that the Jelly scriptlet will be executed whenever the test:test goal is executed. You are also using the waitfor Ant task which waits here for the QOTD web application to be started (you do not want to start executing your test before the QOTD web application is ready to service requests).

Run the tests by executing the test:test goal:

```
C:\dev\mavenbook\code\qotd\acceptance>maven test:test
[...]
test:test:
jetty:prepare-filesystem:

jetty:config:

jetty:run:
     [java] 09:37:54.469 EVENT  Checking Resource aliases
     [java] 09:37:54.619 EVENT  Starting Jetty/4.2.17
     [java] 09:37:54.639 WARN!! Delete existing temp dir C:\DOCUME~1\[...][/
qotd-web,jar:file:/C:/Documents%20and%20Settings/[...]/.maven/repository/
mdn/wars/qotd-web-1.0.war!/]
     [java] 09:37:54.709 EVENT  Started WebApplicationContext[/qotd-web,jar:
file:/C:/Documents%20and%20Settings/[...]/.maven/repository/mdn/wars/qotd-
web-1.0.war!/]
     [java] 09:37:54.729 EVENT  jsp: init
     [java] 09:37:54.820 EVENT  default: init
     [java] 09:37:54.820 EVENT  invoker: init
     [java] 09:37:54.850 EVENT  Started SocketListener on 0.0.0.0:8081
     [java] 09:37:54.850 EVENT  Started org.mortbay.jetty.Server@117a8bd
     [java] 09:37:55.380 EVENT  QuoteServlet: init
    [junit] Testsuite: mdn.qotd.acceptance.QuoteServletTest
    [junit] Tests run: 1, Failures: 0, Errors: 0, Time elapsed: 1,122 sec
    [junit] ------------- Standard Error -----------------
    [junit] 26 mars 2005 09:37:56 org.apache.commons.httpclient.
HttpMethodBase processRedirectResponse
    [junit] INFO: Redirect requested but followRedirects is disabled
    [junit] ------------- ---------------- ---------------
```

```
     [junit]
     [junit] Testcase: testMainServletPage took 0,852 sec
BUILD SUCCESSFUL
Total time: 5 seconds
```

What just happened?

In the last two labs you have been able to set up automated functional tests of a web application using the HtmlUnit test framework, the Maven Jetty plug-in, and the Maven Test plug-in. You should notice also that you have not had to write code or define much of the process.

What about...

...not hardcoding the 8081 port in QuoteServletTest?

You are right. Hardcoding has to be avoided at all costs! One good solution is to pass the port you've defined in the maven.jetty.port property as a System property to the JUnit test. To do this you would need to make the following changes:

- Modify the QuoteServletTest to use this maven.jetty.port property:

```
String port = System.getProperty("maven.jetty.port", "80");
URL url = new URL("http://localhost:" + port + "/qotd-web");
```

- Add the following property to *acceptance/project.properties* so that the Test plug-in can pass the maven.jetty.port property value to your JUnit TestCase:

```
maven.junit.sysproperties = maven.jetty.port
```

Building All Subprojects Simultaneously

Now that you have seen how to split a project into subprojects and how to build each of them individually, let's talk about building them all at once, in the correct dependency order.

How do I do that?

The Multiproject plug-in produces a project dependency graph that allows it to execute any goal on any project under its control. The best way to use the Multiproject plug-in is to set up a master Maven project. This master project is usually set up at the top level of the project directory structure. In the case of the QOTD web application, this means creating top-level *project.xml*, *maven.xml*, and *project.properties* files (see Figure 3-7).

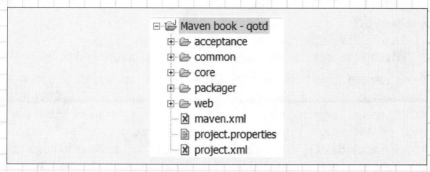

Figure 3-7. Directory structure with top-level project files (maven.xml, project.properties, and project.xml)

This top-level Maven project is a project like any other, except that it doesn't have any source directory. The *project.xml* file extends the *common/project.xml* file, as do the other subprojects:

```
<?xml version="1.0"?>
<project>
  <extend>${basedir}/common/project.xml</extend>
  <artifactId>qotd</artifactId>
  <name>QOTD</name>
  <shortDescription>Quote Of The Day Webapp</shortDescription>
  <description>
    Sample Webapp displaying a Quote Of The Day
  </description>
```

The Multiproject plug-in offers a `multiproject:goal` goal which executes the goal specified by the Maven `goal` property on all the subprojects it can find. For example, executing `maven multiproject:goal -Dgoal=clean` will execute the `clean` goal on all subprojects. However, before executing this command you need to tell the Multiproject plug-in which projects are considered subprojects. You configure this through Maven properties. Three properties control the list of projects to include/exclude, and their default values are as follows:

`maven.multiproject.basedir=${basedir}`

This property represents the location from which the plug-in will look for Maven projects. (In practice, the Multiproject implementation looks for *project.xml* files. When it finds one, it knows it has found a Maven project.)

```
maven.multiproject.includes=*/project.xml
```
This property defines which Maven project to include. The default value says to look for all *project.xml* files located in any directory directly under the top-level directory.

```
maven.multiproject.excludes=
```
This is the counterpart of the `maven.multiproject.includes` property. It says which project to exclude from the multiproject build.

If you wanted to tell the Multiproject plug-in to look for all *project.xml* files located in any directory depth under the top-level directory, you would write `maven.multiproject.includes=**/project.xml` (this follows the Ant pattern syntax; see *http://ant.apache.org/manual/dirtasks. html* for more details). Note that the `**/project.xml` pattern would also match the top-level *project.xml* file. You would not want this, as it would create a circular loop. Thus, you would need to exclude the top-level *project.xml* by specifying `maven.multiproject.excludes=project.xml`.

For the QOTD web application project, you want to exclude the *common/ project.xml* file because it's not a real Maven project and you don't want the Multiproject plug-in to start building it! Your top-level *project. properties* file should be:

```
maven.multiproject.includes=*/project.xml
maven.multiproject.excludes=common/project.xml
```

With these properties set, execute the command `maven multiproject: goal -Dgoal=clean`:

```
C:\dev\mavenbook\code\qotd>maven multiproject:goal -Dgoal=clean

 __  __
|  \/  |__ _Apache__ ___
| |\/| / _` \ V / -_) ' \   ~ intelligent projects ~
|_|  |_\__,_|\_/\___|_||_|  v. 1.0.2

build:start:

multiproject:projects-init:
    [echo] Gathering project list
Starting the reactor...
Our processing order:
QOTD Core
QOTD Web
QOTD Acceptance Tests
QOTD Packager
+------------------------------------------
| Gathering project list QOTD Core
| Memory: 3M/4M
+------------------------------------------
+------------------------------------------
| Gathering project list QOTD Web
```

```
| Memory: 3M/4M
+----------------------------------------
+----------------------------------------
| Gathering project list QOTD Acceptance Tests
| Memory: 3M/4M
+----------------------------------------
+----------------------------------------
| Gathering project list QOTD Packager
| Memory: 3M/4M
+----------------------------------------
Starting the reactor...
Our processing order:
QOTD Core
QOTD GUI
QOTD Acceptance Tests
QOTD Packager
+----------------------------------------
| Executing clean QOTD Core
| Memory: 3M/4M
+----------------------------------------
[...]
```

As you can see, the Multiproject plug-in has automatically discovered the right project build order: QOTD Core, QOTD Web, QOTD Acceptance Tests, and QOTD Packager. The processing order is listed twice because the Multiproject plug-in gathers the project list using a Maven Jelly tag called the reactor for both the projects-init goal and the goal specified in -Dgoal=clean. In a second step, the Multiproject plug-in executes the goal specified on all the projects; in this case, clean is executed on all sub-projects.

TIP

You may have noticed the "3M/4M" memory usage in the preceding code. The first number is the memory used and the second number is the total memory available. They are displayed because there were memory problems in the past, and this was a way to track them. Most of the leaks due to Maven itself have been fixed. However, some due to external libraries still remain, but as Maven continues to mature, you are unlikely to encounter these memory leaks.

Creating Custom Top-Level Goals

Now let's build the QOTD web application using our master project. Hold on! What does it mean to build the QOTD web application? Each subproject has its own definition of *build*: for the core subproject it means calling the jar:install goal, for the web subproject it means calling the war:install goal, etc. You need to define some common goals in your subprojects that you can call from your master project.

How do I do that?

You can do this easily, by creating a *maven.xml* file in each subproject and defining a custom goal in there. Let's call this goal qotd:build. Here's what you would put in the *core/maven.xml* file:

To manage different types of subproject builds, define the same custom goal in each subproject and use the Multiproject plug-in to execute it.

```
<?xml version="1.0"?>

<project default="qotd:build">
  <goal name="qotd:build" prereqs="jar:install"/>
</project>
```

The same applies for the other subprojects. For example, for the web subproject, you'll write:

```
<?xml version="1.0"?>

<project default="qotd:build">
  <goal name="qotd:build" prereqs="war:install"/>
</project>
```

Now that each subproject has a qotd:build goal that builds it, you can also create a qotd:build goal in the master project's *maven.xml* file. This goal uses the Multiproject plug-in to call the qotd:build goal on all the subprojects:

```
<?xml version="1.0"?>

<project default="qotd:build"
    xmlns:j="jelly:core">

  <goal name="qotd:build">
    <j:set var="goal" value="qotd:build"/>
    <attainGoal name="multiproject:goal"/>
  </goal>

  <goal name="qotd:clean" prereqs="multiproject:clean,clean"/>

</project>
```

TIP

Maven 2 is multiproject-aware at its core, and calling a goal on a parent project will automatically call it on all the subprojects. In addition, it supports the notion of build lifecycle (compile, install, deploy, etc.) and plug-ins can bind goals to these different phases. As a consequence, there's no longer a need for custom top-level goals.

To build the full QOTD project, execute the qotd:build goal, and execute maven with no arguments, since the qotd:build goal is defined as the default goal in *maven.xml*:

```
C:\dev\mavenbook\code\qotd>maven
[...]
Starting the reactor...
Our processing order:
QOTD Core
QOTD Web
QOTD Acceptance Tests
QOTD Packager
+-----------------------------------------
| Executing qotd:build QOTD Core
| Memory: 3M/4M
+-----------------------------------------
[...]
+-----------------------------------------
| Executing qotd:build QOTD Web
| Memory: 4M/7M
+-----------------------------------------
[...]
+-----------------------------------------
| Executing qotd:build QOTD Acceptance Tests
| Memory: 5M/7M
+-----------------------------------------
[...]
+-----------------------------------------
| Executing qotd:build QOTD Packager
| Memory: 6M/7M
+-----------------------------------------
[...]
BUILD SUCCESSFUL
Total time: 13 seconds
```

You may have noticed that the top-level *maven.xml* file also contains a useful qotd:clean goal. It directly uses one existing Multiproject plug-in goal called multiproject:clean. It also calls the clean goal because the master project is not in the multiproject includes list.

What about...

...using the existing multiproject:install goal to automatically build all subprojects and install their artifacts?

This is indeed a possibility. In order to use it you would need to define each subproject's type using the maven.multiproject.type property. Some valid types are jar (the default), war, ear, and plugin. When you call multiproject:install, the Multiproject plug-in calls the ${maven.multiproject.type}:install goal for each subproject. This means you could possibly define custom project types and provide a corresponding custom goal in your project's *maven.xml* file. In the QOTD case, the acceptance subproject does not generate any artifact, so you would have needed to define a qotd:install goal that simply ran the acceptance tests. As the packager subproject also contains custom build logic to generate the zip file artifact, you would also have needed to define a qotd: install goal that creates the zip file.

All in all it's sometimes better to create your own qotd:build goals, for the following reasons:

Always try to minimize the size of your maven.xml files.

- The qotd:build goals tell your build users what goals they are supposed to be running. As you know, Maven provides hundreds of available goals, and without these custom goals new users might get a bit lost as to what goal they should execute to build your project.
- The multiproject:install goal is nice if you only have projects that generate artifacts. But in practice, projects do all sort of things when they are built, and producing artifacts is only one aspect of the build.

However, don't overdo it! Remember that Maven is here so that you don't have to maintain a build code. Try reusing existing plug-in goals as much as possible.

Generating a Multiproject Web Site

Now that you know how to build all your projects, let's build a master web site containing content from all the different subprojects' web sites. Indeed, as you know, each Maven project can generate its web site by executing the Site plug-in. However, in the case of your master project, calling maven site would not aggregate the web sites from the different subprojects it is made of.

How do I do that?

Fortunately, the Multiproject plug-in is here to help once again. It has a goal called multiproject:site which you can use to generate this master web site. Let's run it by typing maven multiproject:site. The generated site is located in *target/docs/index.html*. As you can see in Figure 3-8, one of the generated pages is the project overview page, which lists the web sites for all the subprojects.

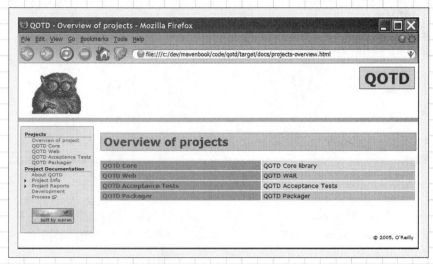

Figure 3-8. Generated multiproject web site showing the overview page

You can decide not to have an overview page if you wish, or you can customize it by playing with the following properties (the default values are shown here):

```
maven.multiproject.overviewPage.create=true
maven.multiproject.overviewPage.title=Overview of projects
maven.multiproject.overviewPage.link=projects-overview
maven.multiproject.overviewPage.linkTitle=Overview of project
maven.multiproject.overviewPage.text=
```

Note that the value of maven.multiproject.overviewPage.text would be displayed between the overview page title and the table listing the subprojects.

You can also choose to have an "independent" navigation. This means that the menu links to the different subproject will point to the URL mentioned in each project's POM url element. As a consequence, you'll also need to publish the different web sites separately (see Chapter 5 for web site deployment). You set this up by setting the maven.multiproject. navigation=independent property (it defaults to aggregate).

CHAPTER 4

Project Reporting and Publishing

Maven is a project comprehension tool at heart. Its general goal is to wrap existing project sources and make sense of them by providing different views. In this chapter you will learn about several Maven plug-ins that help provide visibility for project stakeholders and users. You'll play with plug-ins providing four types of visibility:

- Visibility on project content
- Visibility on project quality
- Visibility on project progress
- Visibility on project deliverables

Throughout this chapter's labs you will reuse the Quote of the Day (QOTD) web application multiproject you created in Chapter 3. You'll use it as a test bed for discovering how to add visibility to a Maven project.

Reporting on Project Content

It is useful to provide visibility on project content, such as mailing lists used, the development team, the Source Control Management (SCM) repository used, the project dependencies, and more.

How do I do that?

The XDoc plug-in automatically generates project information by parsing the Project Object Model (POM). Let's take the qotd/core subproject. Typing maven xdoc (also called if you run maven site) generates Figure 4-1, where you can see the following four reports:

Mailing Lists

> The different mailing lists used by the project. They are defined in the POM using the `mailingLists` tag (see "Telling Maven About Your Team" in Chapter 1).

Project Team

> The members of the teams, and their roles. They are defined in the POM using the `developers` and `contributors` tags (see "Telling Maven About Your Team" in Chapter 1).

Dependencies

> A list of external dependencies used by the project. They are defined in the POM using the `dependencies` tag (see "Adding a Dependency" in Chapter 1).

Issue Tracking

> A link to the issue tracker used by the project. It is defined in the POM using the `issueTrackingUrl` tag.

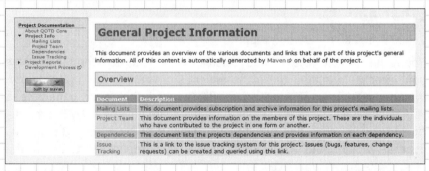

Figure 4-1. The four project information reports generated by the XDoc plug-in

Figure 4-2 shows the Dependencies report for `qotd/core`. It provides interesting information for people who want to use your project, as they can see at a glance what dependencies they'll be using.

Dependencies

The following is a list of dependencies for this project. These dependencies are required to compile and run the application:

Artifact ID	Type	Version	URL
jdom	jar	1.0	http://www.jdom.org/
rome	jar	0.5	http://rome.dev.java.net/

Figure 4-2. Dependencies report for the qotd/core project

Note that the URL field is computed from the optional `url` tag that you can define in a `dependency` tag:

```
<dependency>
  <groupId>rome</groupId>
  <artifactId>rome</artifactId>
  <version>0.5</version>
  <url>http://rome.dev.java.net/</url>
</dependency>
```

It is also useful to ask Maven to generate HTML pages for the source code (main sources and test sources). You'll see in the rest of this chapter that several other reports are automatically linked to these HTML pages. You generate these reports by adding the JXR plug-in's report to the `reports` section of your project's POM. Add it to *qotd/core/project.xml*:

```
<reports>
  <report>maven-jxr-plugin</report>
</reports>
```

What about...

...other project information reports?

You could use the License and Linkcheck plug-ins. The former displays your license (specified using the `maven.license.licenseFile` property, which defaults to *${basedir}/LICENSE.txt*) and the latter generates a report listing all the broken links in the web site generated by the execution of `maven site`. You add them to your POM by adding the `maven-license-plugin` and `maven-linkcheck-plugin` report elements in the `reports` section of your POM.

Reporting Testing Status

Good tests are a major step toward quality software. How do you make this information visible? Two solutions come to mind: sharing a test execution report and showing how much of your code is covered by your tests.

How do I do that?

Let's use the `qotd/core` subproject as a guinea pig for adding a test execution report. Let's add a failing test in addition to the existing one (`testGenerate`) to see what happens in that case. Add the following test to the *qotd/core/src/test/mdn/qotd/core/QuoteGeneratorTest.java* class:

```
public void testBadTestToShowReportingInCaseOfFailure()
{
    assertEquals("Hello Quote!", new QuoteGenerator().generate());
}
```

Add the test report to the *qotd/core/project.xml* reports section:

```
<reports>
    <report>maven-junit-report-plugin</report>
</reports>
```

Let's generate the test report by executing maven site. The generated report is in *qotd/core/target/docs/junit-report.html*, shown in Figure 4-3.

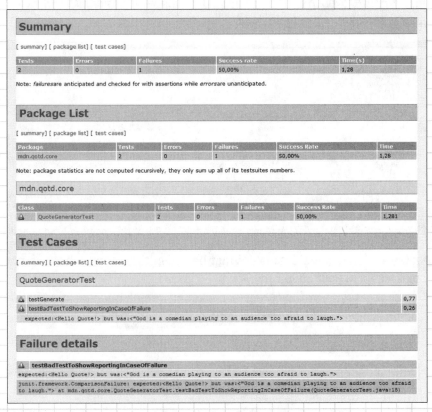

Figure 4-3. JUnit test report showing number of tests and test results

That's good… but it's not enough! This report will show to your users how many tests you have, and their success rate. However, it does not say anything about how good your tests are and whether they properly test your application. For that you need to run a test coverage tool. Fortunately, several are available (including Clover, JCoverage, and Emma), and they all have Maven plug-ins.[*]

---

[*] We have chosen to cover the Clover plug-in because it has the most features and probably the best Maven integration. You should know that Clover is commercial software (although it's free for open source projects), JCoverage has a GPL version, and Emma is open source and free under a CPL license.

Let's use Clover by simply adding the Clover report to the `reports` section in *qotd/core/project.xml*:

```
<reports>
  <report>maven-clover-plugin</report>
  [...]
```

Run maven site and check the generated Clover reports in *qotd/core/target/docs/clover/index.html*. Figure 4-4 shows the summary of what your tests cover of the main code.

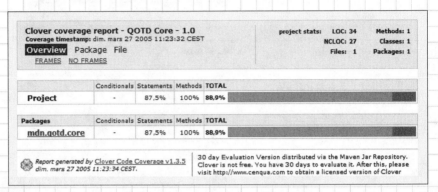

Figure 4-4. Total test coverage report showing that 88.9% of the code has been tested

Figure 4-5 shows the details of what has been tested and what has not been tested in your main code.

Source file	Conditionals	Statements	Methods	TOTAL
QuoteGenerator.java	-	87,5%	100%	**88,9%**

```
1    package mdn.qotd.core;
2
3    import java.net.URL;
4
5    import com.sun.syndication.feed.synd.SyndContent;
6    import com.sun.syndication.feed.synd.SyndEntry;
7    import com.sun.syndication.feed.synd.SyndFeed;
8    import com.sun.syndication.io.SyndFeedInput;
9    import com.sun.syndication.io.XmlReader;
10
11   public class QuoteGenerator
12   {
13       private static final String QUOTE_URL = "http://www.quotationspage.com/data/qotd.rss";
14
15   2     public String generate()
16       {
17   2       SyndFeed quoteFeed;
18   2       try
19         {
20   2         SyndFeedInput input = new SyndFeedInput();
21   2         quoteFeed = input.build(new XmlReader(new URL(QUOTE_URL)));
22         }
23         catch (Exception e)
24         {
25   0         throw new RuntimeException("Failed to get RSS Quote Feed [" + QUOTE_URL + "]", e);
26         }
27
28   2       SyndEntry firstQuoteEntry = (SyndEntry) quoteFeed.getEntries().get(0);
29   2       SyndContent firstQuoteContent = (SyndContent) firstQuoteEntry.getContents().get(0);
30
31   2       return firstQuoteContent.getValue();
32       }
33
34   }
```

Figure 4-5. Details of what has and hasn't been tested

Chapter 4: Project Reporting and Publishing

You can see in the left gutter how many times the code has been executed, and you can see the code that has not been tested. Here it means you have never tested the case when the Really Simple Syndication (RSS) feed cannot be retrieved (when you're offline, for example). This tells you where you should focus your testing effort in the future...

What about...

...the real quality of the tests?

Indeed, test coverage measures do not fully represent the quality of the tests. They just say what part of the code has been covered by the tests. It can happen that a test is wrong, or tests nothing. There is a nice tool called Jester (*http://jester.sourceforge.net*) which performs incremental mutations on the source code and verifies if the test catches the introduced differences. Then it reports what the tests are really testing. The idea is great, but the tool doesn't have a Maven plug-in yet. You know what you have to do now! That would be a good exercise once you finish reading this book...

Reporting on Code Best Practices

When you're working in a team it's good to define development best practices to be used by all the developers. That's great, but how do you enforce their usage? Code reviews? Nah, that's the old way of doing it! Nowadays there are powerful tools to help verify that best practices are applied throughout the code. Some of these tools include Checkstyle (*http://checkstyle.sourceforge.net/*), PMD (*http://pmd.sourceforge.net/*), and Findbugs (*http://findbugs.sourceforge.net/*).* Let's discover how to use the Checkstyle plug-in.

How do I do that?

Add a Checkstyle report to the qotd/core project's POM:

```
<reports>
  <report>maven-checkstyle-plugin</report>
  [...]
```

If you run maven site now you'll get a Checkstyle report, as shown in Figure 4-6. Notice that the cells in Line column can be clicked. They are

---

* There's a list of other verification tools at *http://pmd.sourceforge.net/similar-projects.html*.

links to the JXR report described earlier, showing the code lines causing the violation.

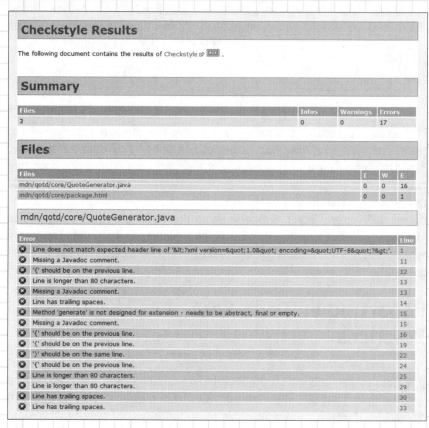

Figure 4-6. Typical Checkstyle report

You may wonder where the rules to apply have been defined. By default the Checkstyle plug-in uses a default configuration file. However, it's very unlikely it'll match your project's coding conventions. You'll need to customize it by adding a property in *qotd/core/project.properties*, pointing to a Checkstyle XML configuration file:

```
maven.checkstyle.properties = ${basedir}/../common/checkstyle.xml
```

TIP

Don't forget that you must use ${basedir} if you want it to work when building the site using the Multiproject plug-in. This is because the Multiproject plug-in is executed from the top-level directory in *qotd/*, and without ${basedir} it'll look for the *checkstyle.xml* file in the wrong place.

It's a good idea to put the *checkstyle.xml* configuration file in *common/*, as you'll share this file with all the QOTD subprojects. Here's a snippet of a typical *checkstyle.xml* file:

```xml
<?xml version="1.0"?>
<!DOCTYPE module PUBLIC
    "-//Puppy Crawl//DTD Check Configuration 1.1//EN"
    "http://www.puppycrawl.com/dtds/configuration_1_1.dtd">

<module name="Checker">
  <module name="TreeWalker">
    <module name="AbstractClassName"/>
    <module name="AvoidStarImport"/>
    <module name="ReturnCount"/>
    <module name="GenericIllegalRegexp">
      <property name="format" value="System\.(out|err)\."/>
      <property name="message"
          value="Don't write directly to System.out our System.err"/>
    </module>
  [...]
```

The full descriptions of all checks are available on the Checkstyle web site (*http://checkstyle.sourceforge.net*). The four checks listed earlier perform the following checks:

- Verify that abstract class names start with the Abstract keyword
- Verify that imports are qualified and do not use the some.package.* shorthand notation
- Verify that methods returning a value have a single return point
- Verify that System.out and System.err are not used

Checkstyle provides hundreds of checks, and it's also possible to write your own extensions.

This is nice, but is it useful? The short answer is no! Reporting on best practices that are not applied does not make the code better. The best solution is to sort the different checks and categorize them by severity with your team. As you can see in Figure 4-6 in the Files table, Checkstyle supports three types of severity checks: errors (E column), warnings (W column), and infos (I column). For example, to have the AvoidStarImport rule as a warning, define it as follows in *checkstyle.xml*:

```xml
<module name="AvoidStarImport">
  <property name="severity" value="warning"/>
</module>
```

Then make the build fail for the error category. You do this by setting the maven.checkstyle.fail.on.violation property to true:

```
maven.checkstyle.fail.on.violation = true
```

What about...

...using PMD?

PMD and Checkstyle are very similar. Each tool has rules that the other does not have, so using both of them makes sense. Using PMD with Maven is very simple: add the `maven-pmd-plugin` report to the `reports` section of the POM.

And what about using Findbugs?

It's a nifty tool in the same category as Checkstyle and PMD. However, it's even more focused toward finding semantic errors than syntactic ones. You are really encouraged to use it in addition to Checkstyle and Maven. You'll be surprised by its findings! To use it with Maven, add `maven-findbugs-plugin` to your reports. However, you must install the Findbugs plug-in first—it's not part of the Maven distribution. You can find it at *http://maven-plugins.sourceforge.net/repository/maven-plugins/plugins/*. Refer to or Chapter 6 to learn how to install a Maven plug-in.

You may also want to investigate JDepend (*http://www.clarkware.com/software/JDepend.html*) and JavaNCSS (*http://www.kclee.de/clemens/java/javancss/*). These tools also have Maven plug-ins to help you assert the quality of your code.

Reporting on Duplicate Code

You should avoid code duplication like the plague! It's very insidious: you fix a bug and you think you're done. Unfortunately, this is not always true, as one developer may have copied/pasted in the past the buggy part you have just fixed. Fortunately, code duplication tools are available, and they have Maven plug-ins. Let's explore how to use the CPD (which stands for Copy Paste Detector) and Simian (*http://www.redhillconsulting.com.au/products/simian/*) tools.*

How do I do that?

CPD is actually part of the PMD project, and it's contained in the Maven PMD plug-in. To use it, start by adding `maven-pmd-plugin` to the `reports` section of the POM. Then tell the plug-in to generate the CPD report by adding the following property to your project's *project.properties* file:

```
maven.pmd.cpd.enable = true
```

---

* Simian is a commercial product, but you can get free licenses for noncommercial/nongovernment projects. Simian has a 15-day evaluation period.

Figure 4-7 shows a typical CPD report.

```
CPD Report

===================================================================
Found a 12 line (115 tokens) duplication in the following files:
Starting at line 76 of C:\dev\cargo\core\container\src\main\org\codehaus\cargo\container\resin\AbstractResinContainer.java
Starting at line 107 of C:\dev\cargo\core\container\src\main\org\codehaus\cargo\container\resin\AbstractResinContainer.java
    java.setFork(true);
    java.addSysproperty(getAntUtils().createSysProperty("resin.home",
        getConfiguration().getDir()));
    Path classpath = java.createClasspath();
    classpath.createPathElement().setLocation(getResourceUtils().getResourceLocation("/"
        + ResinRun.class.getName().replace('.', '/') + ".class"));
    FileSet fileSet = new FileSet();
    fileSet.setDir(getHomeDir());
    fileSet.createInclude().setName("lib/*.jar");
    classpath.addFileset(fileSet);
    java.setClassname(ResinRun.class.getName());
    java.createArg().setValue("-stop");
```

Figure 4-7. Typical CPD report showing duplicate lines

By default CPD reports duplicates that share more than 100 tokens. To configure it differently use the `maven.pmd.cpd.minimumtokencount` Maven property. For example, to detect duplicates of 50 tokens or more, use this:

```
maven.pmd.cpd.minimumtokencount = 50
```

Just as with code best practice detection, the duplicate reports are not very helpful when it comes to fixing the code. A better strategy is to set a high duplicate threshold and fail the build if duplicates are found. Then, as your project progresses, slowly decrease the duplicate threshold to uncover more and more duplicates. Of course, there's a minimum threshold that you'll have to find out (say, around 5–10 lines). Unfortunately, the PMD plug-in does not yet support failing the build upon duplicate detection.

Now let's use the Simian plug-in, which has such a feature. Start by adding `maven-simian-plugin` to your project's `reports` section. Then add the following property:

```
maven.simian.failonduplication = true
```

Running the Simian plug-in on the same project as the one in Figure 4-7 leads to the report shown in Figure 4-8.

Clicking any duplication link leads to a page showing the duplicated source code. You can configure the duplication threshold using the `maven.simian.linecount` property. There are other interesting properties in the Simian plug-in reference documentation (*http://maven.apache.org/reference/plugins/simian/properties.html*).

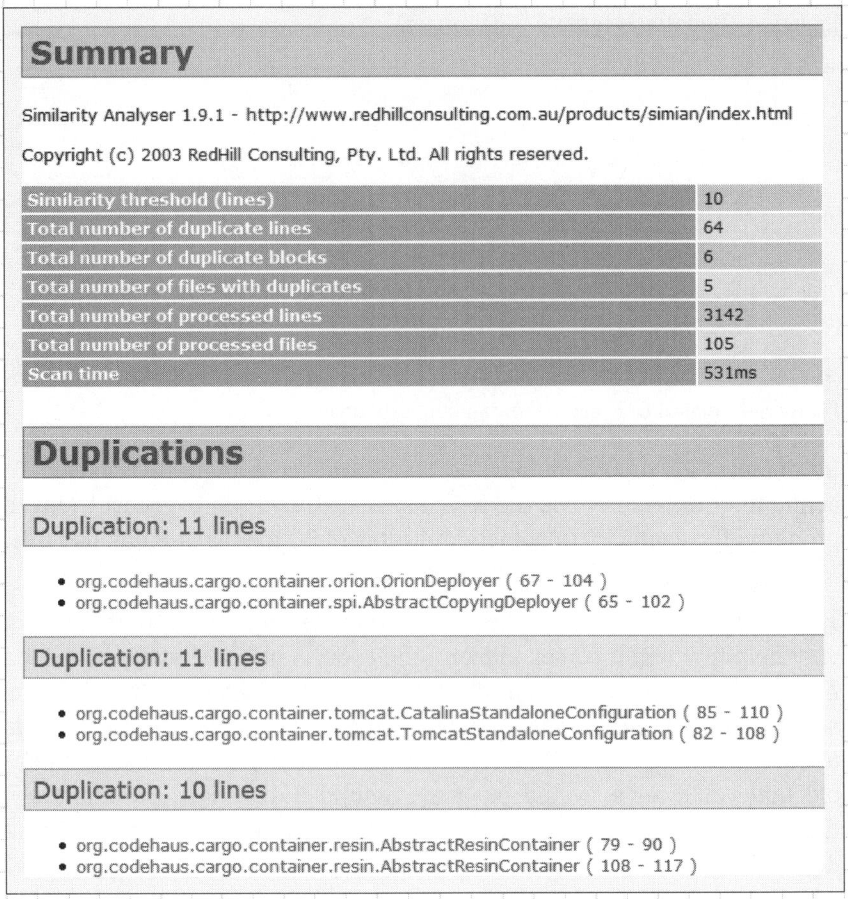

Summary

Similarity Analyser 1.9.1 - http://www.redhillconsulting.com.au/products/simian/index.html

Copyright (c) 2003 RedHill Consulting, Pty. Ltd. All rights reserved.

Similarity threshold (lines)	10
Total number of duplicate lines	64
Total number of duplicate blocks	6
Total number of files with duplicates	5
Total number of processed lines	3142
Total number of processed files	105
Scan time	531ms

Duplications

Duplication: 11 lines

- org.codehaus.cargo.container.orion.OrionDeployer (67 - 104)
- org.codehaus.cargo.container.spi.AbstractCopyingDeployer (65 - 102)

Duplication: 11 lines

- org.codehaus.cargo.container.tomcat.CatalinaStandaloneConfiguration (85 - 110)
- org.codehaus.cargo.container.tomcat.TomcatStandaloneConfiguration (82 - 108)

Duplication: 10 lines

- org.codehaus.cargo.container.resin.AbstractResinContainer (79 - 90)
- org.codehaus.cargo.container.resin.AbstractResinContainer (108 - 117)

Figure 4-8. Typical Simian report

Generating a Quality Dashboard

You've seen how to generate some quality reports, such as a testing report, a test coverage report, a best practice violations report, and duplicate code reports. There are actually lots of other Maven reports related to quality (for instance, JavaNCSS, JDepend, and JCoverage, to name a few). Having all those reports generated is great, but it's a bit difficult to get a clear picture of the overall quality of a project. In addition, all these plug-ins generate reports for single projects and not multiprojects. How do you get aggregated quality reports that span a complete multiproject?

How do I do that?

In the previous labs you added reports to the qotd/core subproject. Now you'll use the Maven Dashboard plug-in to provide quality visibility to the full QOTD multiproject.

Add the `maven-dashboard-plugin` report to the `reports` section in your master project's POM. For the QOTD multiproject this is the *qotd/project.xml* file. Now tell the Dashboard plug-in what subprojects to include in the report. By default the Dashboard plug-in uses the values from the following three multiproject properties, seen in Chapter 3 and shown here with their default values:

```
maven.multiproject.basedir = ${basedir}
maven.multiproject.includes = */project.xml
maven.multiproject.excludes =
```

In the case of the QOTD multiproject, these default values are fine because all the subprojects are matching the */project.xml pattern.

The Dashboard plug-in introduces the notion of *aggregators*. An aggregator represents a metric. More than 25 aggregators are available. Here are some examples:

cserrors
> Computes the total number of Checkstyle errors

clovertpc
> Computes the total Test Coverage Percentage (TPC) using Clover

simiantdl
> Computes the total number of duplicate lines found by Simian

javancssncsstotal
> Computes the total number of noncommented source statements as computed by JavaNCSS

The aggregators to display in the Dashboard report are controlled by the `maven.dashboard.aggregators` property. The default aggregators included in the report are:

```
maven.dashboard.aggregators = cserrors,cswarnings,clovertpc,cloverloc,cloverncloc
```

Running `maven site` on the master project in *qotd/* generates the report in Figure 4-9.

By default the Dashboard plug-in executes the necessary goals to generate the reports that the aggregators are relying on (Checkstyle, Clover, etc.) before extracting the metrics and aggregating them in the master

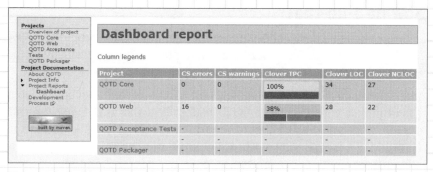

Figure 4-9. Dashboard report for the QOTD multiproject

project's report, as shown in Figure 4-9. That makes it very easy to run the Dashboard plug-in, but it's not always the most efficient way. If the subprojects already generate some of the individual reports aggregated by the Dashboard, these reports will be executed several times, wasting some precious build time.

Fortunately, the Dashboard plug-in supports a mode that integrates well with the `multiproject:site` goal and lets each subproject generate its individual reports. Start by asking the Dashboard report not to generate the individual reports itself, by adding the following properties to your *qotd/project.properties* file:

```
maven.dashboard.runreactor = false
maven.dashboard.rungoals = false
```

Now tell the Multiproject plug-in to call the `dashboard:report-single` goal for each subproject. You do this by setting the `maven.multiproject.site.goals` property in *qotd/project.properties*:

```
maven.multiproject.site.goals = site,dashboard:report-single
```

The `dashboard:report-single` goal creates a *${maven.build.dir}/dashboard-single.xml* file in each subproject, containing the aggregator metrics. The Dashboard plug-in gathers all the individual *dashboard-single.xml* files to produce the master report for all subprojects.

For this to work, you'll of course need to ensure that each subproject has the correct reports defined in the `reports` section of their POMs. The Dashboard report will now be generated when you run *maven multiproject:site*.

What just happened?

You have discovered how to use some Maven plug-ins that will improve your intrinsic code quality. You have also discovered how to report the violations found. However, very often, simply reporting is not enough, and failing the build in case of violation should be preferred. In the next lab we'll discuss how to provide visibility about project activity.

What about...

...drawing history graphs?

You're right, that would be fabulous, but the Dashboard plug-in doesn't support this yet. Actually, the Dashboard plug-in has probably grown to the point where it should be made a separate, Maven-independent project. It could be similar to Checkstyle, PMD, Clover, and other similar projects. Then you could refactor the Dashboard plug-in to use this external Dashboard project.

Don't be a report maniac! Prefer quality checks that fail the build over nice reports that nobody pays attention to....

TIP

Best practice: don't write too much code that isn't purely build-related in *maven.xml* or Maven plug-ins. If you find yourself doing this, consider externalizing the non-build-related code in a separate Java project, and refactor your Jelly code to use it instead.

Tracking Project Activity

Tracking a project's activity is very important for end users/stakeholders. Several good indicators are available that can aid in tracking:

- The number of commits per day
- The number of additional unit tests added every day
- The evolution of test percentage coverage
- The mailing list activity
- The number of existing books on the project (mostly for open source projects)
- The number of committers
- The number of open issues in the project's bug tracker
- The number of years the project has been in existence

It would be very nice to have the equivalent of the Dashboard plug-in, but for project activity. This could provide a global project activity score à la SourceForge project activity percentage (e.g., *http://sourceforge.net/ project/stats/?group_id=15278*).* Unfortunately, such a comprehensive plug-in does not yet exist! Instead, you have several ad hoc possibilities:

- Use the StatCVS-XML plug-in to analyze a CVS repository and generate statistics.† Unfortunately, such a tool doesn't exist for Subversion yet, but it won't be long before one does.

- Use the Developer-Activity and File-Activity Maven plug-ins that respectively report on developer commits and files containing the most changes, within a given date range.

Let's discover how to use these plug-ins.

How do I do that?

To use the StatCVS-XML plug-in you must install it, as it's not part of the default Maven distribution. Install the plug-in from *http://statcvs-xml. berlios.de/*, following the installation steps described in the   and in Chapter 6. You'll also need to ensure you have a command-line CVS client installed, as the plug-in is using the Ant cvs task to gather CVS logs for your project.

Using the plug-in cannot be simpler: add the maven-statcvs-plugin report to the reports section of your project's POM and run maven site. Myriad reports are generated, but here are a few that you should know more about in order to understand a project's activity. Figure 4-10 shows the commit activity per author and the aggregated activity over the whole lifetime of the Jakarta Cactus project.

Another very interesting report shows changes brought to a project over time, module by module, as shown in Figure 4-11 for the StatCVS-XML project itself.

The goal here is not to take you through a full-length tutorial of StatCVS-XML, but rather to show you its power and how you can integrate it in a

---

* SourceForge's current ranking formula is: log (3 * # of forum posts for that week) + log (4 * # of tasks ftw) + log (3 * # bugs ftw) + log (10 * patches ftw) + log (5 * tracker items ftw) + log (# commits to CVS ftw) + log (5 * # file releases ftw) + log (.3 * # downloads ftw).

† Unfortunately, no such tool exists for Subversion—but it won't be long before one does.

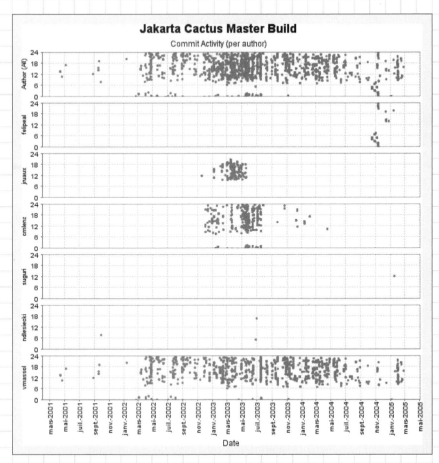

Figure 4-10. Commit activity over time

Maven project. You are strongly encouraged to explore it on your own at *http://statcvs-xml.berlios.de/*.

Although StatCVS-XML generates developer and file activity reports, it's still interesting to find out how to use the Developer-Activity and File-Activity plug-ins, as they also support Subversion. To use them, simply add them as usual to your POM. Let's do that on *qotd/core/project.xml*:

```
<reports>
  <report>maven-developer-activity-plugin</report>
  <report>maven-file-activity-plugin</report>
  [...]
```

Running maven site generates the reports shown in Figure 4-12 and Figure 4-13.

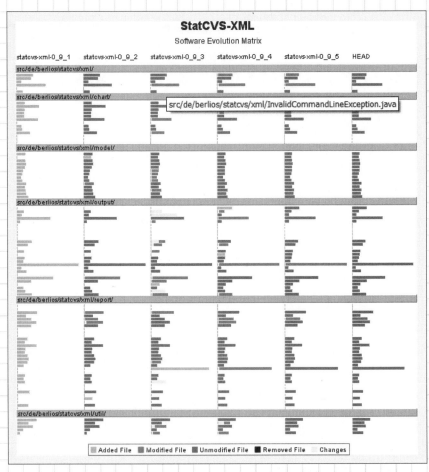

Figure 4-11. Changes to the StatCVS-XML project over time, module by module

Figure 4-12. Developer activity showing number of commits and files modified

Both of these reports internally use the Changelog plug-in that you'll learn about in the next lab. You can configure them by using Changelog plug-in properties, such as the maven.changelog.range property that controls the report timeframe.

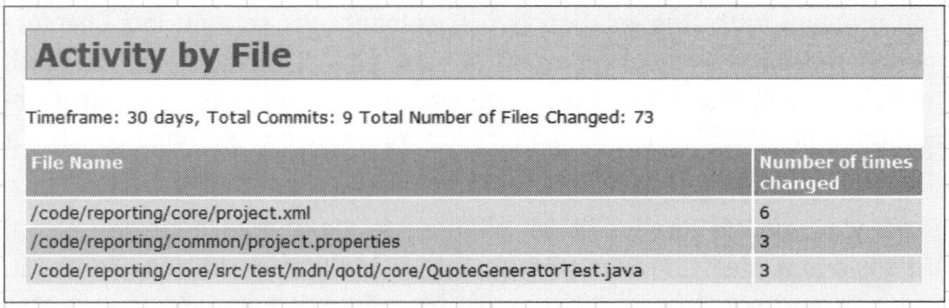

Activity by File

Timeframe: 30 days, Total Commits: 9 Total Number of Files Changed: 73

File Name	Number of times changed
/code/reporting/core/project.xml	6
/code/reporting/common/project.properties	3
/code/reporting/core/src/test/mdn/qotd/core/QuoteGeneratorTest.java	3

Figure 4-13. Files which have been changed recently, ordered by change frequency

Tracking Project Changes

When you're developing a project, it's useful to provide to your users a list of changes between the previous version of the project and the current version. This allows users who are expecting a feature or a bug fix to verify that the enhancement is in the new version. But even more important is the fact that you can regularly publish the progress report, which will keep your users and/or stakeholders spellbound!

How do I do that?

The first solution that comes to mind is to use the Maven Changelog plug-in. It extracts commit logs from your SCM and generates a report. It has a `maven.changelog.range` property that controls how many days in the past to look when performing the extraction. To use it, add it to your `reports` section in *qotd/core/project.xml*:

```
<reports>
  <report>maven-changelog-plugin</report>
  [...]
```

After executing `maven site` you'll get a report similar to the one in Figure 4-14.

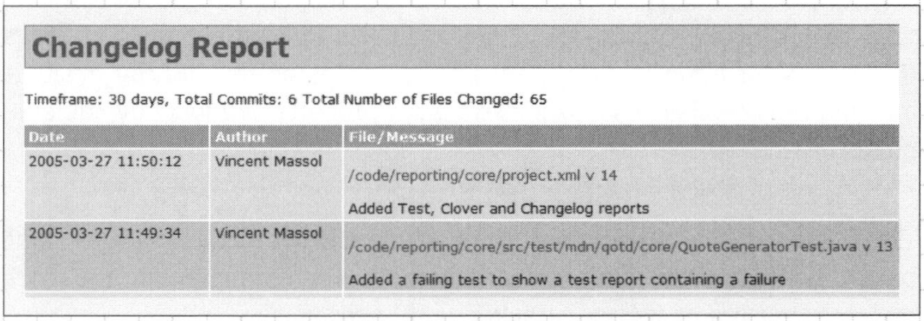

Changelog Report

Timeframe: 30 days, Total Commits: 6 Total Number of Files Changed: 65

Date	Author	File/Message
2005-03-27 11:50:12	Vincent Massol	/code/reporting/core/project.xml v 14 Added Test, Clover and Changelog reports
2005-03-27 11:49:34	Vincent Massol	/code/reporting/core/src/test/mdn/qotd/core/QuoteGeneratorTest.java v 13 Added a failing test to show a test report containing a failure

Figure 4-14. Sample Changelog report showing the last 30 days' worth of SCM commits

The problem with this solution is that commit logs contain lots of information that is not useful for users of your project. Actually, showing all those logs will make it close to impossible for anyone to find out user-related changes. Automatic generation of relevant changes is still a dream!

Thus, you need to hand-edit the changes to make them nice and clean. Maven has a nice Changes plug-in that helps you to do this. To use it, create a *qotd/core/xdocs/changes.xml* file with the following format (this is an example):

```
<?xml version="1.0" encoding="UTF-8"?>

<document>
  <properties>
    <title>Changes</title>
  </properties>
  <body>
    <release version="1.0-SNAPSHOT" date="in SVN">
      <action dev="vmassol" type="update">
        Restricted the changelog report to only show the changes for the
        last week.
      </action>
    </release>
    <release version="0.9" date="2005-03-22" description="Initial release">
      <action dev="vmassol" type="fix" issue="QOTDCORE-1">
        The changelog report now works with Subversion.
      </action>
      <action dev="vmassol" type="add">
        Initial release. See the features page for more details.
      </action>
    </release>
  </body>
</document>
```

Each `release` tag corresponds to a version release and each change is described using the `action` tag. An action can be an addition (type="add"), a removal (type="delete"), an update (type="update"), or a bug fix (type="fix"). As you can see from the preceding code snippet, with the QOTDCORE-1 issue it's also possible to link an action to an issue URL from your issue tracker. The plug-in computes the URL by evaluating the `maven.changes.issue.template` property which, by default, points to:

```
maven.changes.issue.template = %URL%/%ISSUE%
```

The %URL% token is the value of the `issueTrackingUrl` tag in *project.xml*, but without the last element in the path. For example, for the `core` project using Jira as its issue tracker, you have:

```
<project>
  [...]
```

```
<issueTrackingUrl>
  http://www.mavenbook.org/jira/browse/QOTDCORE
</issueTrackingUrl>
[...]
```

The %ISSUE% token is the issue number defined in the action tag of
changes.xml (QOTDCORE-1 here). Thus, the full URL that is computed by
the Changes plug-in is:

```
http://www.mavenbook.org/jira/browse/QOTDCORE-1
```

TIP

If you're using a bug tracker that doesn't match the default issue
template, you'll need to modify the value of maven.changes.
issue.template. For example, for Bugzilla you would use:

```
maven.changes.issue.template =
    %URL%/show_bug.cgi?id=%ISSUE%
```

And you would use:

```
maven.changes.issue.template =
    http://sourceforge.net/support/tracker.php?aid=%ISSUE%
```

for the SourceForge tracker.

Add the maven-changes-plugin report to your POM reports section and
execute maven site to generate the report shown in Figure 4-15.

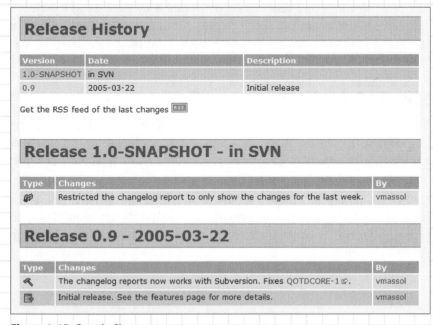

Figure 4-15. Sample Changes report

One nice additional bonus is that the Changes report generates an RSS feed of the changes. Thus, your project users can add this feed in their favorite Feed Aggregator (SharpReader, FeedDemon, BlogLines, Newz Crawler, etc.), and they'll know right away whenever a change is made!*

What about...

...using issue tracking software for change logs?

This is a very good solution that more and more projects are adopting. You'll need to practice what we (the authors) call Issue Driven Development (IDD) to make it work. IDD goes like this: when a task is done, and just before the code is checked in, ensure that a corresponding issue exists in your issue tracker. If there's no issue for this task, create one (unless the modification is a really minor one that the user should not be concerned with). Then, check in the code mentioning the issue number in the check-in comment, and close/resolve the issue. The result of using IDD is that you can ask your issue tracker to generate a representative change log because all the important changes have an associated issue.

Publishing Maven Artifacts

The previous labs covered how to add project visibility on quality and progress. Now let's add visibility on deliverables by publishing a project's artifacts. Let's consider the QOTD project. It has several artifacts: a JAR in *qotd/core*, a WAR in *qotd/web*, and a zip in *qotd/packager*. Imagine you want to deploy them to a Maven remote repository.

How do I do that?

Several Maven plug-ins—including the JAR, WAR, EAR, and RAR plug-ins—deploy the artifact they generate. Thus, to deploy a JAR you use `jar:deploy`, to deploy a WAR you use `war:deploy`, to deploy an EAR you use `ear:deploy`, etc.

Under the hood all these deploy goals use the Artifact plug-in's `artifact:deploy` Jelly tag to perform the actual deployment. Thus, to properly deploy an artifact you need to find out how to configure the Artifact plug-in.

* See Vincent's blog post about Source Code Communication at *http://tinyurl.com/exbsb*.

Let's practice by deploying the *qotd/core* JAR. The first thing to decide is what deployment protocol you're going to use. The Artifact plug-in supports several deployment protocols: SCP, file copy, FTP, and SFTP (see *http://maven.apache.org/reference/plugins/artifact/protocols.html* for more details).

You are going to use the SCP method to deploy the JAR artifact, as it is one of the most commonly used protocols, and it's secure. You also need to tell the Artifact plug-in where to deploy to. Let's imagine you'd like to publish to *www.mavenbook.org*, for example.

As these properties are true for any subproject in QOTD, add the following Artifact plug-in properties to *common/project.properties*:

```
maven.repo.list = mavenbook

maven.repo.mavenbook = scp://www.mavenbook.org
maven.repo.mavenbook.directory = /var/www/html/mavenbook/maven
```

Deployment properties are defined for the mavenbook deployment repository using the following syntax: maven.repo.[repository name].*, where [repository name] is mavenbook. maven.repo.list is a comma-separated list containing all the repositories to deploy to, and in this case you are publishing to only one remote repository—mavenbook. The maven.repo. mavenbook property defines both the protocol to use (SCP here) and the deployment host. maven.repo.mavenbook.directory specifies the deployment directory on the host server.

You also need to specify deployment credentials. It's best to define those in a *build.properties* file, as this file is not meant to be checked in your SCM and you want your password to remain secret. If your deployment server uses username/password authentication, you'll define:

```
maven.repo.mavenbook.username = vmassol
maven.repo.mavenbook.password = somepassword
```

TIP

Simply define the following properties:

```
maven.repo.mavenbook = ftp://www.mavenbook.org
maven.repo.mavenbook.directory = /var/www/html/mavenbook/maven
maven.repo.mavenbook.username = vmassol
maven.repo.mavenbook.password = somepassword
```

to publish using FTP.

If your SSH server supports private key authentication, you can use the maven.repo.mavenbook.privatekey and maven.repo.mavenbook.passphrase

Unfortunately, you won't be able to publish to mavenbook.org. If you want to try this, you'll need your own SSH server. Sorry!

properties instead of a password. A more secure approach is to configure an authentication key for SSH in a user account on the machine you want to deploy from.

The Artifact plug-in uses the JSch framework (*http://www.jcraft.com/jsch/*) under the hood for supporting the SSH protocol. You'll get the following kind of stack trace error:

```
com.jcraft.jsch.JSchException: Auth fail
        at com.jcraft.jsch.Session.connect(Unknown Source)
        at org.apache.maven.deploy.deployers.
GenericSshDeployer...
```

if you have not configured authentication correctly.

Publish the core JAR artifact:

```
C:\dev\mavenbook\code\reporting\core>maven jar:deploy
[...]
jar:deploy:
    [echo] maven.repo.list is set - using artifact deploy mode
Will deploy to 1 repository(ies): mavenbook
Deploying to repository: mavenbook
Deploying: C:\dev\mavenbook\code\reporting\core\project.xml-->mdn/poms/qotd-
core-1.0.pom
Executing command: mkdir -p /var/www/html/mavenbook/maven/mdn/poms

Executing command: chmod g+w /var/www/html/mavenbook/maven/mdn/poms/qotd-
core-1.0.pom

Deploying: C:\dev\mavenbook\code\reporting\core\project.xml.md5-->mdn/poms/
qotd-core-1.0.pom.md5
Executing command: mkdir -p /var/www/html/mavenbook/maven/mdn/poms

Executing command: chmod g+w /var/www/html/mavenbook/maven/mdn/poms/qotd-
core-1.0.pom.md5

Will deploy to 1 repository(ies): mavenbook
Deploying to repository: mavenbook
Deploying: C:\dev\mavenbook\code\reporting\core\target\qotd-core-1.0.jar-->
mdn/jars/qotd-core-1.0.jar
Executing command: mkdir -p /var/www/html/mavenbook/maven/mdn/jars

Executing command: chmod g+w /var/www/html/mavenbook/maven/mdn/jars/qotd-
core-1.0.jar

Deploying: C:\dev\mavenbook\code\reporting\core\target\qotd-core-1.0.jar.
md5-->mdn/jars/qotd-core-1.0.jar.md5
Executing command: mkdir -p /var/www/html/mavenbook/maven/mdn/jars
```

```
Executing command: chmod g+w /var/www/html/mavenbook/maven/mdn/jars/qotd-
core-1.0.jar.md5

BUILD SUCCESSFUL
```

What just happened?

The `artifact:deploy` tag is executing commands on the remote machine
using SSH. The structure of the repository is being created, and all directories and files are made group-writable with `chmod`. As you can see from
the console, the `artifact:deploy` tag has deployed not only the `core`
JAR, but also the `core` project's POM. This is because the POM is the
identity of a Maven project and it may be useful for a user browsing the
repository to know more about the project producing the artifacts he's
looking for. In practice the POMs will also enable Maven 2 to support
transitive dependencies. This means that in the future you'll be able to
specify only the direct dependencies your project is depending upon, and
Maven will auto-discover the dependencies of your dependencies.

Transitive dependencies are going to be a huge timesaver.

Because you can never be too security conscious, the `artifact:deploy`
tag creates MD5 signatures for every deployed artifact. Maven currently
does not use them when downloading artifacts, but they'll certainly be
implemented in the future.

What about...

...publishing the `packager`'s zip file?

Publishing the JAR was easy because there's an existing `jar:deploy`
goal. However, there's no zip plug-in, and thus no `zip:deploy` goal! The
solution is to write a custom goal in your *maven.xml* file. Edit the *qotd/
packager/maven.xml* file and add the code in bold:

```
<?xml version="1.0"?>

<project default="qotd:build"
    xmlns:ant="jelly:ant"
    xmlns:artifact="artifact">

  <goal name="qotd:build">
    <ant:mkdir dir="${maven.build.dir}"/>
    <ant:zip destfile=
        "${maven.build.dir}/${pom.artifactId}-${pom.currentVersion}.zip">
      <ant:fileset file="${pom.getDependencyPath('mdn:qotd-web')}"/>
      <ant:fileset dir="${maven.src.dir}/conf"/>
    </ant:zip>
  </goal>
```

```
<goal name="qotd:deploy" prereqs="qotd:build">
  <artifact:deploy
      artifact="${maven.build.dir}/${pom.artifactId}-${pom.currentVersion}.zip"
      type="zip"
      project="${pom}"/>
</goal>

  </project>
```

The qotd:build goal creates the QOTD zip (see Chapter 3 for a refresher).
You've now added a qotd:deploy goal that uses the artifact:deploy
Jelly tag to deploy the zip file, and then passed in the artifact attribute.
The type attribute corresponds to the artifact extension that is used to
decide in which directory to put the artifact in the remote repository. You
need to pass a reference to the current project's POM in the project
attribute. Running qotd:deploy deploys the zip to the remote repository,
in *[REMOTE_REPO_ROOT]/mdn/zips/qotd-packager-1.0.zip*, following the
standard repository mapping rule, [REPO_ROOT]/<groupId>/<type>s/
<artifactId>-<currentVersion>.<type>, discussed in Chapter 1.

Announcing a Project Release

You have deployed your artifacts to a Maven remote repository. Now you
need to announce this fact to your project stakeholders.

How do I do that?

Use the Announcement plug-in. If you've been following the practice of
using a *changes.xml* file to describe your project changes, as demon-
strated earlier, this will be very easy. If not, you're out of luck, as the
Announcement plug-in works hand in hand with the Changes plug-in.

In this lab you'll generate a release announcement for the qotd/core
subproject, which will allow you to reuse the *changes.xml* file you added
in a previous lab.

Decide for what release you want to generate the announcement. If you
don't configure anything, an announcement for the current version
defined in the POM will be generated. You can control this through the
maven.announcement.version property, which defaults to:

```
maven.announcement.version = ${pom.currentVersion}
```

The Announcement plug-in makes one check: it verifies that there is a
version tag in the POM that matches the release for which you wish to
generate the announcement. A version tag indicates that a release has

been made, and it's also meant to link the release with the SCM tag that you've used. It's indeed good practice to tag your SCM when performing a software release. Let's imagine that you've already released version 0.9 of the core project. Add the following version information to *qotd/core/project.xml*:

```
[...]
    </repository>

    <versions>
      <version>
        <id>0.9</id>
        <name>0.9</name>
        <tag>QOTD_CORE_0_9</tag>
      </version>
    </versions>
[...]
```

Note that the name element is simply a friendly name for the id tag. It can be whatever you like.

Generate the announcement for release 0.9 by running maven announcement:generate (note that we're passing a property on the command line):

```
C:\dev\mavenbook\code\reporting\core>maven announcement:generate ^
More? -Dmaven.announcement.version=0.9
[...]
announcement:generate:
    [echo] Generating announcement for release 0.9 in C:\dev\mavenbook\code\
reporting\core/target/generated-xdocs/announcements/
announcement-0.9.txt...
    [echo] Using stylesheet located at file:C:\Documents and Settings\
Vincent Massol\.maven\cache\maven-announcement-plugin-1.3\pl
ugin-resources/announcement.jsl and UTF-8 encoding
BUILD SUCCESSFUL
```

You can find the generated announcement in *target/generated-xdocs/announcements/announcement-0.9.txt*:

```
The mdn team is pleased to announce the QOTD Core 0.9 release!

http://www.mavenbook.org/projects/mdn/qotd-core

QOTD Core library

Changes in this version include:

  New Features:

o Initial release. See the features page for more details.

  Fixed bugs:
```

```
o The changelog report now works with Subversion. Issue: QOTDCORE-1.

Have fun!
-The mdn team
```

As you can see, the Announcement plug-in generated this text by gathering information from the POM and from the *core/changes.xml* file:

```
[...]
    <release version="0.9" date="2005-03-22" description="Initial release">
      <action dev="vmassol" type="fix" issue="QOTDCORE-1">
        The changelog reports now works with Subversion.
      </action>
      <action dev="vmassol" type="add">
        Initial release. See the features page for more details.
      </action>
    </release>
  </body>
</document>
```

What about...

...sending this announcement by email?

You can do that using the `announcement:mail` goal. At a minimum you'll need to tell the plug-in what SMTP server to use and to whom to send the email. You specify the SMTP server by adding the following property in your *build.properties* file (this is indeed a property that depends on your environment and may or may not be shared with others):

```
maven.announcement.mail.server = my_smtp_server
```

The recipients are defined using the `maven.announcement.mail.to` property. For example:

```
maven.announcement.mail.to = users@mavenbook.org,dev@mavenbook.org
```

The plug-in will compute the email sender by looking at the `developers` section of the POM and will use the email of the first developer it finds, unless you have specified a sender using the `maven.announcement.mail.from` property. Several other optional properties exist; you can find them online at *http://maven.apache.org/reference/plugins/announcement/ properties.html*.

Reporting Project Releases

You have published project releases. Now would be a good time to discover how to let your users know where to find them. Let's add a release report to the project web site.

How do I do that?

The XDoc plug-in has a nice feature: it can generate a download report listing all past releases, with a link to the artifacts and the release announcements. Let's use it on the QOTD `packager` project. The `packager` is the project that generates the main QOTD distributable, so it makes sense to have it generate the download report.

First, tell the XDoc plug-in where the artifacts are published. You do this by using the `maven.xdoc.distributionUrl` property. Add it to the *qotd/packager/project.properties* file:

```
maven.xdoc.distributionUrl=http://www.mavenbook.org/maven/mdn/zips/
```

The distribution URL is an important piece of information missing from the POM. It will be added in the near future. The XDoc plug-in needs information about the releases that have been made. It gets this information from the POM by scanning the `version` tags. Let's imagine that you've already released versions 0.7, 0.8, and 0.9 of the `packager` project. Add the following version information to *qotd/packager/project.xml*:

```
[...]
  </repository>

  <versions>
    <version>
      <id>0.7</id>
      <name>0.7</name>
      <tag>QOTD_PACKAGER_0_7</tag>
    </version>
    <version>
      <id>0.8</id>
      <name>0.8</name>
      <tag>QOTD_PACKAGER_0_8</tag>
    </version>
    <version>
      <id>0.9</id>
      <name>0.9</name>
      <tag>QOTD_PACKAGER_0_9</tag>
    </version>
  </versions>
[...]
```

You saw in the previous lab that the Announcement plug-in can generate announcement reports. It would be nice to add them to the download report so that users who want to download your software can know what the download contains. The download report will automatically add the announcement reports if the XDoc plug-in can find a *changes.*

xml file with releases matching the `version` tags of the POM. Add one to *qotd/packager/xdocs/changes.xml*:

```
<?xml version="1.0" encoding="UTF-8"?>

<document>
  <properties>
    <title>Changes</title>
  </properties>
  <body>
    <release version="1.0-SNAPSHOT" date="in SVN">
      [...]
    </release>
    <release version="0.9" date="2005-03-22">
      [...]
    </release>
    <release version="0.8" date="2005-03-10">
      [...]
    </release>
    <release version="0.7" date="2005-03-01">
      [...]
    </release>
  </body>
</document>
```

You're all set! Reap the fruits of your hard labor by typing `maven site`. It'll generate a download report, as shown in Figure 4-16.

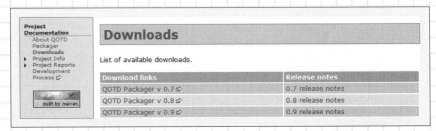

Figure 4-16. Download report showing QOTD packager's releases, including release notes

Note that there is a visible Downloads link in the left menu that draws the attention of visitors.

What about...

...having a Downloads link on the master QOTD web site?

Yes, you're right, the Downloads link in the `packager` project is nice, but it isn't very visible for visitors who will arrive on the top-level site. The solution is to write a *qotd/xdocs/downloads.xml* XDoc document linking to the different subprojects' download reports. Indeed, it's possible that several subprojects produce distributable artifacts and this solution allows you to list them all on the main *downloads.xml* page.

Publishing a Project Web Site

You have generated lots of reports in this chapter. These reports will not do any good if they're not made available by publishing them. Let's remedy this!

How do I do that?

Publishing to a single project web site is different from publishing to a multiproject web site only in terms of the goal to call: you call multiproject:site-deploy for multiprojects and site:deploy for single projects. In practice, the multiproject:site-deploy goal simply starts by calling the multiproject:site goal that we saw in Chapter 3, and then it calls site:deploy on it to upload the site to the remote server.

TIP

At the time of this writing the Site plug-in does not use the Artifact plug-in to deploy the web site as an artifact. This will certainly happen in future versions of Maven, and at that time you'll be able to practice your newly acquired knowledge of publishing project artifacts.

The Site plug-in supports four protocols for deploying a web site: File System (fs), SSH (ssh), FTP (ftp), and RSync (rsync). SSH is the default one, but if you wish to choose another one, define the maven.site. deploy.method property in your properties file (either *project.properties* or *build.properties*, depending on whether you wish to share this property with other team members):

```
maven.site.deploy.method = ssh
```

Let's publish the QOTD web site to *http://www.mavenbook.org/mdn/qotd* using SSH.

To use the SSH method you need to have SSH and SCP clients installed, and the maven.ssh.executable and maven.scp.executable properties must point to them. For example, if you're on Windows and have

installed PuTTY's Plink and Pscp (*http://www.chiark.greenend.org.uk/*
~sgtatham/putty/download.html) and they're in your PATH, you would
write the following in your *build.properties* file:

```
maven.ssh.executable = plink
maven.scp.executable = pscp
```

You also need to specify the username under which you wish to deploy
the site. Specify it in your *build.properties* file. For example:

```
maven.username = vmassol
```

TIP

Most of the problems you will have when publishing a web site
using SSH will be due to authentication. It's strongly recommended
to use a public/private key scheme. If you don't use one, your SSH
executable will want to prompt you to enter the password but
Maven will not propagate this prompt. It'll thus appear to hang. You
should always use your SSH client first to ensure you can connect to
the remote host automatically, without having to type anything.

Now you need to tell the Site plug-in where to deploy to by defining the
siteAddress and siteDirectory elements in the QOTD POM. As these
properties are shared by all subprojects, define them in *qotd/common/
project.xml*:

```
[...]
  <url>http://www.mavenbook.org/projects/${pom.groupId}/${pom.artifactId}</url>

  <siteAddress>www.mavenbook.org</siteAddress>
  <siteDirectory>
    /var/www/html/mavenbook/projects/${pom.groupId}/${pom.artifactId}
  </siteDirectory>
[...]
```

Publish the QOTD web site by typing multiproject:site-deploy:

```
C:\dev\mavenbook\code\reporting>maven multiproject:site-deploy
[...]
site:local-deploy-init:
    [echo]
      site clean = false
      siteDirectory = /var/www/html/mavenbook/projects/mdn/qotd


site:remote-deploy-init:
    [echo]
      siteAddress = www.mavenbook.org
      siteUsername = vmassol
```

```
site:sshdeploy:
    [tar] Building tar: C:\dev\mavenbook\code\reporting\target\qotd-1.0-
site.tar
    [gzip] Building: C:\dev\mavenbook\code\reporting\target\qotd-1.0-site.
tar.gz
    [delete] Deleting: C:\dev\mavenbook\code\reporting\target\qotd-1.0-site.
tar
[...]
```

Open a browser and point it to *http://www.mavenbook.org/mdn/qotd*.
Enjoy!

What about...

...using another deployment method?

Refer to the Site plug-in reference documentation at *http://maven.
apache.org/reference/plugins/site/*. For example, to use the FTP protocol
you would use the same properties as defined earlier, and simply tell the
site:deploy goal that you're using FTP by setting the following:

```
maven.site.deploy.method = ssh
```

CHAPTER 5

Team Collaboration with Maven

You have already discovered how to use Maven locally on your development machine. However, when you're working on a team, new issues arise:

- How do I share my build environment with the other team members so that we are all sure we are using the same build configuration?
- How do I ensure that my work integrates well with other modules developed by other team members, and if they don't, how can I be warned quickly to correct them?
- How do I ensure that the work that I commit to the team's Source Control Management (SCM) system does not prevent others from working, even though I may have introduced errors causing build failures?

These are natural questions that you will have to face and answer when working on a team. In this chapter you'll explore real-world strategies to deal with these issues, and you'll apply these strategies using Maven and CruiseControl.

Sharing a Maven Installation

When you're working on a team, it's a good idea to use a common development environment. This way you don't have to constantly struggle to figure out why something that works on your machine doesn't work on that of a colleague. A common development environment also makes it easier to upgrade dependencies and add new features to your shared build and test systems. A common challenge in large workgroups is standardizing on a central build system, and in this lab, you will discover how to share a Maven installation on a development team.

How do I do that?

The first thing to do is to unpack the Maven installation files and place them in a location accessible by everyone. Typically, this can be either a shared drive or an SCM system (in the latter case developers will need to check out the Maven files). A good practice is to make this shared Maven installation read-only; this makes it impossible for developers to introduce errors into files not intended for modification. Let's assume that you now have access to the shared Maven installation files from the *c:\apps\ maven* directory on a Windows machine, or from the */usr/local/maven* directory in a Unix environment (you can pick any directory you like).

Now, set your MAVEN_HOME environment variable to point to *c:\apps\ maven* (or */usr/local/maven* on Unix) and have your PATH environment variable point to MAVEN_HOME/bin. Figure 5-1 shows a Maven installation shared between two users—Vincent and Tim.

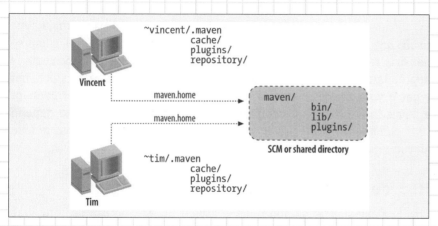

Figure 5-1. Sharing a Maven installation between two development members (Vincent and Tim)

What just happened?

You have just shared a Maven installation. The core Maven files are the same ones used by everyone, and all your user-specific local Maven files are located on your machine in a *.maven* directory located in your home directory. Your *.maven* directory contains the following subdirectories:

- The *cache/* directory, which contains all the Maven plug-ins found in *MAVEN_HOME/plugins* in expanded format (they are JAR files). You can safely delete this directory, and Maven will re-create it at the next run.

In Maven 2 there's no longer a notion of unpacking plug-in JARs, nor of a cache directory. Plug-ins are accessed directly from the repository.

- The *plugins/* directory, which is the user plug-in directory. Maven does not create this directory automatically. You can create it if you need to use custom plug-ins. Any JAR plug-in that you drop in this directory will be expanded by Maven in the *cache/* directory. Note that in the case of a version conflict, the plug-ins in this *plugins/* directory take precedence over the plug-ins in *MAVEN_HOME/ plugins*. Using the *plugins/* directory is a good way to customize a read-only Maven installation.

- The *repository/* directory, which was explained in Chapter 1. This directory is your local Maven repository and it contains all the artifacts that are cached locally on your machine.

Creating Your Own Remote Maven Repository

By default, when you install Maven, it is configured to use *http://www. ibiblio.org/maven* as the remote repository; ibiblio provides a comprehensive selection of free and open source artifacts. This repository is appropriate if you're developing a free and open source product, but what if your project needs to depend on either commercial artifacts or artifacts internal to your company? For example, if you need to depend on a commercial JDBC driver, you will need to set up your own remote Maven repository.

How do I do that?

This is really simple: all you need is a web server. You can use any web server you like, be it Apache, Tomcat, Microsoft IIS, etc. The only recommendation is that it supports the if-modified-since HTTP header (but we think they all do!), as this is the internal mechanism used by Maven to decide whether an artifact needs to be downloaded to your local repository.

Let's use Tomcat. Download it from *http://jakarta.apache.org/site/ downloads/downloads_tomcat.html* (at the time of this writing the latest version available in the 4.x series was Tomcat 4.1.31). Install it anywhere you wish—say, in *C:\apps\jakarta-tomcat-4.1.31* if you're on Windows—and start it using *bin/startup.bat* (for Windows) or *bin/startup.sh* (for Unix). By default, Tomcat will start on port 8080. If you're already using this port, edit the *config/server.xml* file and modify the port. Verify that you have it working by opening a browser and typing *http://localhost:8080* (you should also try to access it from another machine using `http://[hostname]:8080`).

Now, create the repository directory. Go in *webapps/ROOT* (this directory will be created the first time you start Tomcat). It is mapped to the / context, which means that this is the directory served when you type *http://localhost:8080*. Create a subdirectory called *repository/*. This will be our remote Maven repository location which will be accessed with the *http://localhost:8080/repository* URL. You should have a directory structure similar to the one in Figure 5-2. Now you can copy any artifact in your newly created remote repository. Its directory structure is the same as that of your local repository.

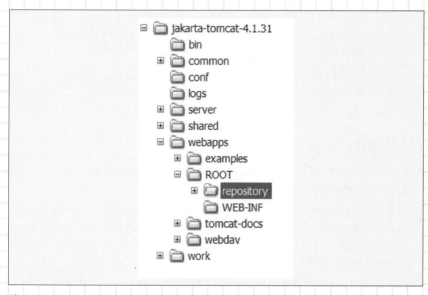

Figure 5-2. Your new remote Maven repository showing proper directory structure

Now that you have your new remote repository set up, let's discover how to use it for your Maven projects. A Maven property named `maven.repo.remote` controls where Maven looks for its remote repository. It is hardcoded to be *http://www.ibiblio.org/maven* by default. There are several recommended places where you could change it:

- In your *~user/build.properties* file
- In a *build.properties* file in your project's directory
- In your project's *project.properties* file if you wish to share this location with other team members

Modify your *build.properties* file so that it contains the following line:

```
maven.repo.remote = http://[hostname]:8080/repository
```

You can also specify more than one remote repository. Maven will try to find the artifacts in the first repository. If it doesn't find them, it will look in the second repository, etc. For example, if you wish to define your own repository in addition to ibiblio, you would write:

```
maven.repo.remote = http://[hostname]:8080/repository, http://www.ibiblio.org/maven
```

If your project needs to use a commercial artifact, such as a commercial JDBC driver from Oracle, you would put that commercially licensed product's JAR files in your own remote repository and continue to use the ibiblio Maven repository for open source dependencies.

TIP

Some well-known JARs in the Java world, such as activation, javamail, jaxp, jca, jdbc, and jndi, are used by lots of projects. You might be surprised not to find them on ibiblio. The reason is that their licensing does not allow for their redistribution*. Putting them in your own remote repository is thus a very good idea.

What just happened?

You have discovered how to create your own Maven remote repository by hand. There are three ways you can use it:

- As a placeholder for your own private artifacts (i.e., all artifacts that cannot be found on ibiblio). In this case you would usually define a `maven.repo.remote` property pointing to both your private remote repository and the ibiblio one.

- As a way to control all the artifacts that are allowed. In this case, you would define a single remote repository in your `maven.repo.remote` property (your private repository). You would populate it manually with all the artifacts from ibiblio that you need. Whenever a new artifact is required by a project you would add it to your remote repository. This strategy is well suited for companies that wish to control the artifacts they have in their remote repositories.

---

* The Maven development team is trying to develop an agreement with Sun Microsystems that would allow publishing these JARs into ibiblio (see *http://maven.apache.org/project/ sun-licensing-journey.html* for more details).

- As a brute force approach to caching an existing remote repository (such as ibiblio). A more evolved solution would be to use maven-proxy (*http://maven-proxy.codehaus.org/*).

What about...

...momentarily disabling the remote repository to work in offline mode?

If you're on the road or simply if you don't have network or Internet access, you can tell Maven to work in offline mode by running Maven with the -o option (maven -o <goals>) or by setting the maven.mode. online property to false. We mentioned this in Chapter 1, but it is such a common question we thought we'd bring it up again. If you need to use Maven while disconnected from the Internet, use the -o flag, and Maven will not attempt to connect to any remote repositories. Be aware that in this case Maven will only use the artifacts present in the local repository, and the build will fail if a required dependency is not there.

If you are working in a café without WiFi, use the -o flag to work "off-line."

Setting Up a Continuous Integration Build

An easily reproducible build and testing system allows your development team to focus on coding rather than some complex and error-prone build tool based on a specific local environment. Using a build container such as Maven also reduces the amount of tedious work involved in setting up everyone's local build environment. When you're working in a team, developers will commit code to the SCM only after they have verified that their changes are appropriately tested and that their local build passes. In reality, there are several reasons why a local build would pass on your machine but fail on another developer's: you could have forgotten to update your working copy before committing, you could be using a different database instance, etc. What you'd like to do is find out as quickly as possible if the code that everyone commits is working. A bug introduced by one developer may be an obstacle to another developer's progress, and ideally, you want to build and test a system after each commit so that you can identify problems as they occur. This is known as Continuous Integration.[*]

---

[*] See Martin Fowler's reference article on Continuous Integration (*http://www.martinfowler. com/articles/continuousIntegration.html*).

How do I do that?

The best solution found so far is to set up what is called a Continuous Integration build. You're going to do that now using Maven and CruiseControl (*http://cruisecontrol.sourceforge.net/*). You're going to set up a continuous build for the Quote of the Day (QOTD) web application introduced in Chapter 3.

The architecture is simple (see Figure 5-3) and is composed of three entities

Developer workstations

This is where developers commit code changes to the SCM.

SCM repository

You are going to use the Subversion repository where we have stored the web application source code. The only thing you'll need for this is an Internet connection that allows HTTP on port 80 (this should be a pretty common setup!). Note that CruiseControl supports a host of SCMs (Subversion, CVS, ClearCase, CM Synergy, Starteam, VSS, Surround, etc.).

CruiseControl server

This is a server which continuously polls the SCM to see if there are changes, and if so, it starts a Maven build to build the QOTD project, generate build logs, publish build results (send email, deploy artifacts to a web site, etc.), and make them available for viewing through the CruiseControl web application.

Let's go through the following steps:

1. Install CruiseControl on your machine.

2. Install the Subversion command-line client.

3. Create a work directory for the QOTD project's build and check out the qotd project from Subversion.

4. Modify the qotd project so that you can use the Maven CruiseControl plug-in to generate a valid CruiseControl configuration.

5. Start CruiseControl.

6. Make a change to a file in the SCM and observe CruiseControl rebuilding the project.

7. Configure the CruiseControl web application and view the build results.

For the sake of simplicity you'll run CruiseControl on your local machine for this lab. However, you would normally install CruiseControl on a separate server machine.

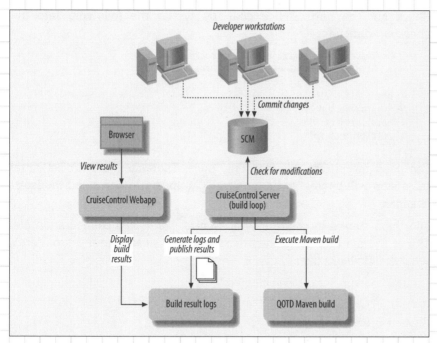

Figure 5-3. The Continuous Integration build architecture using CruiseControl and Maven

To install CruiseControl, download it from *http://cruisecontrol. sourceforge.net/* and unzip it to a convenient place on your hard drive. Let's imagine you wish to have it in *c:/apps/cruisecontrol-.2.2.1* (we used version 2.2.1 for this lab). Add *c:/apps/cruisecontrol-2.2.1/main/bin* to your PATH environment variable so that you can later type cruisecontrol on the command line to start the CruiseControl server.

Now let's install the Subversion command-line client, as it will be required by CruiseControl and by Maven for performing SCM actions (such as updating the files, performing a checkout, etc.). Download it from *http://subversion.tigris.org/* and use the package corresponding to your operating system. Make sure that you can type svn from any directory. If not, add to your PATH environment variable the *bin/* directory where the *svn* executable has been installed.

Now we need to set up a work directory where we will put the CruiseControl configuration for the QOTD project. This work directory will also be the location where the Maven build will execute and where CruiseControl will generate its logs. Create the following directory structure:

```
c:/dev/mavenbook/work/cruisecontrol/
  checkout/
  logs/
```

Check out the `qotd` source code by typing the following into the *checkout/* directory:

```
C:\dev\mavenbook\work\cruisecontrol\checkout>svn co ^
More? http://www.mavenbook.org/svn/mdn/code/qotd

A qotd\.classpath
A qotd\project.properties
A qotd\.project
A qotd\project.xml
[...]
```

You need to perform this step only once. Thereafter, the CruiseControl build loop will be able to perform an SCM update to download the latest changes.

Your next step is to create a CruiseControl *config.xml* configuration file. This is the file that completely describes the CruiseControl setup. Here's what the file looks like:

```xml
<?xml version="1.0" encoding="UTF-8"?>

<cruisecontrol>
  <project name="qotd">
    <bootstrappers>
      <currentbuildstatusbootstrapper
          file="c:/dev/mavenbook/work/cruisecontrol/logs/qotd/status.txt"/>
    </bootstrappers>
    <modificationset>
      <svn localWorkingCopy="c:/dev/mavenbook/work/cruisecontrol/checkout/qotd"
          repositoryLocation="http://www.mavenbook.org/svn/mdn/code/qotd"/>
    </modificationset>
    <schedule interval="300">
      <maven goal="scm:update|clean qotd:build"
          projectfile=
              "c:/dev/mavenbook/work/cruisecontrol/checkout/qotd/project.xml"
          mavenscript="c:\apps\maven-1.0.2/bin/maven.bat"/>
    </schedule>
    <log dir=
        "c:/dev/mavenbook/work/cruisecontrol/logs/qotd" encoding="ISO-8859-1">
      <merge dir=
          "c:/dev/mavenbook/work/cruisecontrol/checkout/qotd" pattern="TEST-*.xml"/>
    </log>
    <publishers>
      <currentbuildstatuspublisher
          file="c:/dev/mavenbook/work/cruisecontrol/logs/qotd/status.txt"/>
      <htmlemail spamwhilebroken="false" reportsuccess="always"
          css="C:/apps/cruisecontrol-2.2.1/reporting/jsp/webcontent/css/cruisecontrol.css"
          mailhost="localhost" subjectprefix="[BUILD]"
          buildresultsurl="http://www.mavenbook.org/[...]"
          defaultsuffix="@apache.org" returnaddress="vmassol@apache.org"
          xsldir="C:/apps/cruisecontrol-2.2.1/reporting/jsp/webcontent/xsl"
          logdir=
              "c:/dev/mavenbook/work/cruisecontrol/logs/qotd" skipusers="false">
```

```
        <map address="vmassol@apache.org" alias="vmassol"/>
        <map address="tobrien@apache.org" alias="tobrien"/>
        <failure address="vmassol@apache.org"/>
        <success address="vmassol@apache.org"/>
      </htmlemail>
    </publishers>
  </project>
</cruisecontrol>
```

Don't bother trying to understand the different elements in this file, as
that's not required for this lab. If you want to dive into CruiseControl configuration, check the excellent documentation at *http://cruisecontrol.*
sourceforge.net/main/configxml.html. The point we wish to make here is
that the information found in the CruiseControl configuration file (the
SCM information, the location of Maven home, email addresses, the name
of the project, etc.) can also be found in your project's Project Object
Model (POM). It's a shame to have to duplicate this information in two
separate places. Fortunately, there is an existing CruiseControl plug-in for
Maven that can automatically generate this file for you by using the POM
information and some additional information that you pass to it. Let's use
this plug-in and start by adding the following properties to our *build.*
properties file (because these properties are environment-dependent):

```
maven.cruisecontrol.home = c:/apps/cruisecontrol-2.2.1
maven.cruisecontrol.work.dir = c:/dev/mavenbook/work/cruisecontrol
```

Now add the following two properties to the *qotd/project.properties* file
(this is the master QOTD project's configuration file; see Chapter 3 for a
refresher):

```
maven.cruisecontrol.goals = scm:update|clean qotd:build
maven.cruisecontrol.mail.host = [your SMTP mail server here]
```

Many properties control the CruiseControl plug-in, but these are the four
main ones that are required to get a working CruiseControl configuration
for the QOTD multiproject:

maven.cruisecontrol.home
> This is the location where you have installed CruiseControl on your
> machine.

maven.cruisecontrol.work.dir
> This is your CruiseControl work directory that you created earlier in
> this lab.

maven.cruisecontrol.goals
> This property contains the list of goals that the CruiseControl Maven
> builder will pass to Maven to build the qotd project. The first goal is
> scm:update. It uses the Maven SCM plug-in to perform an SCM

update and download all changes. This is how we ensure that we always build with the latest changes. The pipe symbol (|) is used by the Maven builder to denote a different Maven session. Thus, in practice the Maven builder will call Maven twice: once to run the scm:update goal and once to run the clean and qotd:build goals. The qotd:build goal is the one that you created in Chapter 3 and that builds the full project.

maven.cruisecontrol.mail.host

This is the name of the SMTP server that CruiseControl will use to send failure or success emails.

You'll also need to make sure that you have defined where your SCM is located in your POM (*qotd/project.xml*):

```
<repository>
  <connection>scm:svn:http://www.mavenbook.org/svn/mdn/code/qotd
  </connection>
</repository>
```

Let's try it out and generate the *config.xml* file. Go into the *qotd/* directory and type the following:

```
C:\dev\mavenbook\code\qotd>maven cruisecontrol
[...]
scm:find-connection:
    [echo] Using connection: scm:svn:http://www.mavenbook.org/svn/mdn/code/qotd

scm:parse-connection:
    [echo] Using SCM method: svn
    [echo] Using SVN repository: http://www.mavenbook.org/svn/mdn/code/qotd

scm:validate:

cruisecontrol:validate:

cruisecontrol:configure:
    [mkdir] Created dir: C:\dev\mavenbook\code\qotd\target\cruisecontrol
    [copy] Copying 1 file to C:\dev\mavenbook\code\qotd\target\cruisecontrol
    [delete] Deleting: C:\dev\mavenbook\code\qotd\target\cruisecontrol\
config-temp.xml
BUILD SUCCESSFUL
Total time: 2 seconds
```

This generates a *config.xml* file in *C:\dev\mavenbook\code\qotd\target\ cruisecontrol*. This file needs to be copied to your CruiseControl work directory (remember that the CruiseControl server will run from there). The CruiseControl plug-in has a cruisecontrol:install-local goal for installing the generated configuration in the working directory. Let's run it:

```
C:\dev\mavenbook\code\qotd>maven cruisecontrol:install-local
[...]
cruisecontrol:configure:
    [copy] Copying 1 file to C:\dev\mavenbook\code\qotd\target\cruisecontrol
    [delete] Deleting: C:\dev\mavenbook\code\qotd\target\cruisecontrol\
config-temp.xml

cruisecontrol:install-local:
    [copy] Copying 1 file to C:\dev\mavenbook\work\cruisecontrol
BUILD SUCCESSFUL
Total time: 2 seconds
```

The *config.xml* file has been copied to *c:\dev\mavenbook\work\ cruisecontrol*, which now contains:

```
C:/dev/mavenbook/work/cruisecontrol/
    checkout/
      qotd/
    logs/
    config.xml
```

As you may have noticed the cruisecontrol:install-local goal actually calls the cruisecontrol:configure goal. Thus, whenever you wish to regenerate the CruiseControl configuration file you can do it all in one step by calling cruisecontrol:install-local.

Note that if CruiseControl was installed on another machine you would need to copy the *config.xml* file by another means (possibly using the Ant FTP task or the Ant SCP task).

Now you're ready to turn on CruiseControl. Go to *c:/dev/mavenbook/ work/cruisecontrol* and type cruisecontrol:

```
C:\dev\mavenbook\work\cruisecontrol>cruisecontrol
[...]
[cc]feb.-19 10:37:57 Main        - CruiseControl Version 2.2.1
[cc]feb.-19 10:37:57 trolController- projectName = [qotd]
[cc]feb.-19 10:37:57 trolController- No previously serialized project found:
                                 C:\dev\mavenbook\work\cruisecontrol\qotd
[cc]feb.-19 10:37:57 Project - Project qotd: reading settings from config file
                        [C:\dev\mavenbook\work\cruisecontrol\config.xml]
[cc]feb.-19 10:37:58 Project      - Project qotd starting
[cc]feb.-19 10:37:58 Project      - Project qotd:  idle
[cc]feb.-19 10:37:58 BuildQueue   - BuildQueue started
[cc]feb.-19 10:37:58 Project      - Project qotd started
[cc]feb.-19 10:37:58 Project      - Project qotd: next build in 5 minutes
[cc]feb.-19 10:37:58 Project      - Project qotd: waiting for next time to
                                 build
```

The build sleeps for five minutes. This is the default build schedule interval, which you can change by using the maven.cruisecontrol.schedule. interval property. For example, to set it to one minute:

```
maven.cruisecontrol.schedule.interval = 60
```

After this interval, CruiseControl starts building the qotd project (it always does it the very first time, even if there have been no changes in the SCM):

```
[cc]feb.-19 11:29:20 Project        - Project qotd: in build queue
[cc]feb.-19 11:29:20 BuildQueue     - now adding to the thread queue: qotd
[cc]feb.-19 11:29:20 Project     - Project qotd: reading settings from config file
                            [C:\dev\mavenbook\work\cruisecontrol\config.xml]
[cc]feb.-19 11:29:20 Project        - Project qotd:bootstrapping
[cc]feb.-19 11:29:20 Project        - Project qotd:checking for modifications
[cc]feb.-19 11:29:39 Project        - Project qotd:No modifications found,
                                      build not necessary.
[cc]feb.-19 11:29:39 Project        - Project qotd: Building anyway, since
                                      build was explicitly forced.
[cc]feb.-19 11:29:39 Project        - Project qotd:  now building
build:start:

scm:find-connection:
    [echo] Using connection: scm:svn:http://www.mavenbook.org/svn/mdn/code/qotd

scm:update:
    [echo] Updating from scm:svn:http://www.mavenbook.org/svn/mdn/code/qotd
[INFO] Executing: svn --non-interactive update
[INFO] Working directory: c:\dev\mavenbook\work\cruisecontrol\checkout\qotd
BUILD SUCCESSFUL
Total time: 40 seconds

build:start:

clean:clean:

clean:

qotd:build:
[...]
```

As you can see, the CruiseControl Maven builder has started by calling a Maven session with the scm:update goal, followed by another Maven session with the clean qotd:build goals.

The default CruiseControl configuration you have used sends an HTML email on every build (success or failure):

```
[cc]feb.-19 11:30:37 Project        - Project qotd:  merging accumulated log
                                      files
[cc]feb.-19 11:30:38 Project        - Project qotd:  build successful
[cc]feb.-19 11:30:38 Project        - Project qotd:  publishing build results
[cc]feb.-19 11:30:42 EmailPublisher- Sending mail notifications.
```

Figure 5-4 shows the type of HTML mail you should have received.

The CruiseControl server will then periodically poll your SCM for changes, and if none is found it goes back to sleep:

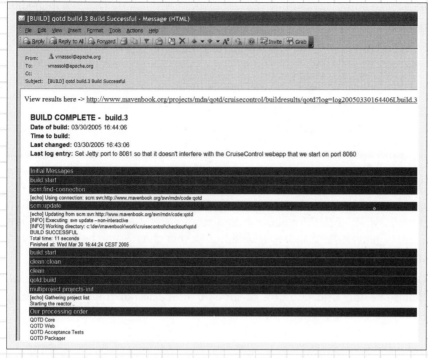

Figure 5-4. HTML email sent by CruiseControl upon build success and/or failure

```
[cc]feb.-19 15:56:23 Project      - Project qotd: idle
[cc]feb.-19 15:56:23 Project      - Project qotd: next build in 5 minutes
[cc]feb.-19 15:56:23 Project      - Project qotd: waiting for next time to
                                      build
[cc]feb.-19 16:01:23 Project      - Project qotd:in build queue
[cc]feb.-19 16:01:23 BuildQueue   - now adding to the thread queue: qotd
[cc]feb.-19 16:01:23 Project      - Project qotd: reading settings from config file
                                      [C:\dev\mavenbook\work\cruisecontrol\config.xml]
[cc]feb.-19 16:01:23 Project      - Project qotd:bootstrapping
[cc]feb.-19 16:01:23 Project      - Project qotd:checking for modifications
[cc]feb.-19 16:01:41 Project      - Project qotd:No modifications found,
                                      build not necessary.
```

The last step of this lab on Continuous Integration is to configure and start the CruiseControl web application, which allows you to browse build results and see some statistics. Grab the *cruisecontrol.war* file located in the *reporting/jsp/dist* directory of your CruiseControl install directory (*c:/apps/cruisecontrol-2.2.1/* in our case). Unfortunately, you need to configure this web application by telling it where the Cruise-Control log directory is located on your hard disk, and this configuration parameter is located... in the *WEB-INF/web.xml* file of the *cruisecontrol. war* file! Fortunately, the CruiseControl Maven plug-in is here to help us once again, and executing the `cruisecontrol:configure-war` goal will generate a properly configured CruiseControl web application WAR:

```
C:\dev\mavenbook\code\qotd>maven cruisecontrol:configure-war
[...]
cruisecontrol:configure-war:
    [unwar] Expanding: C:\apps\cruisecontrol-2.2.1\reporting\jsp\dist\
cruisecontrol.war into C:\dev\mavenbook\code\qotd\target\cruisecontrol\
cruisecontrolwar
    [war] Building war: C:\dev\mavenbook\code\qotd\target\cruisecontrol\
cruisecontrol.war
BUILD SUCCESSFUL
Total time: 3 seconds
```

Drop the generated *c:/dev/mavenbook/code/qotd/target/cruisecontrol/ cruisecontrol.war* file in your favorite `Servlet` container (for Tomcat, drop it in *[TOMCAT_HOME]/webapps*) and start it. See the "Creating Your Own Remote Maven Repository" lab earlier in this chapter for help on how to install/start Tomcat.

Open your browser and point it to *http://localhost:8080/cruisecontrol*. You'll see the CruiseControl dashboard that lists all the projects being built (see Figure 5-5).

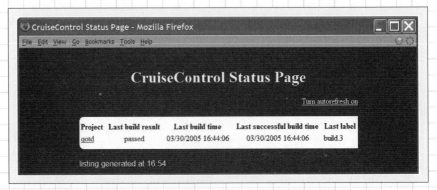

Figure 5-5. CruiseControl dashboard page showing all the projects built by CruiseControl

Click the qotd link to display the build status page for the QOTD project (see Figure 5-6). On the left it shows the list of builds, and in the middle it shows the selected build results. You can see that the shown build was successful, that three unit tests were executed, and that vmassol made one change since the last successful build. This is a very useful feature for finding out why a build breaks.

Chapter 5: Team Collaboration with Maven

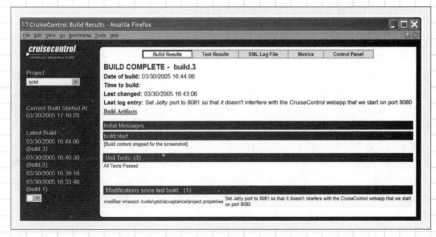

Figure 5-6. CruiseControl build result page for the qotd project

We invite you to explore the different tabs to learn more details about the data gathered by CruiseControl during the build.

What about...

...defining one CruiseControl project per Maven subproject?

That would sound like a sensible approach. However, that would mean letting CruiseControl handle inter-project dependencies. Unfortunately, this is not a strong point of CruiseControl and is best left to Maven's Multiproject feature. In addition, Maven's CruiseControl plug-in does not handle well the use of one CruiseControl project per Maven subproject. At this point in time, we do not recommend using this strategy.

You could use other Continuous Integration tools, such as Gump (*http://gump.apache.org/*), DamageControl (*http://damagecontrol.codehaus.org/*), or Continuum (*http://maven.apache.org/continuum/*). Note that a Gump plug-in is available for Maven that automatically generates a Gump descriptor. However, the tool that has the most support at the time of this writing is certainly CruiseControl, and we highly recommend it.

TIP

At the time of this writing Continuum is still in its infancy. Continuum is a project developed by the Maven team and is targeted primarily at Maven projects. Thus, we expect it to become the preferred Continuous Integration tool for Maven projects in the future.

Using Binary Dependencies

Imagine yourself on a team of several developers with a project made of several Maven subprojects. When you wish to build the Maven subproject you're working on you have two choices: start by building all its dependencies using the Multiproject plug-in (see Chapter 3) or directly build the said subproject assuming that the dependencies have already been built and are available in your Maven remote repository. The first strategy uses source dependencies (in the sense that you build the dependencies from the sources) and the second strategy uses binary dependencies. The latter is very useful on medium to large projects where building all dependent projects on each developer's machine would take too long. It's also extremely useful when you have several teams, each developing a subset of the full application; each team can concentrate on its own code and release the code as a binary artifact to the other teams. This lab will teach you how to set up a binary dependency strategy.

How do I do that?

You know how to create your own remote repository, how to set up a continuous build, and how to deploy project artifacts. Now you have all of the ingredients necessary for implementing a binary dependencies strategy.

Let's go through the architecture of a binary dependencies build strategy (see Figure 5-7) to see what we need to set up:

- The continuous build runs all the time and builds all subprojects. Whenever it has finished building a project and if the build was successful, it deploys the subproject's artifacts to the Maven remote repository.
- When you build a project, Maven checks the list of its dependencies defined in the *project.xml* file and verifies if the dependencies are available in the local repository.
- In the case of *SNAPSHOT* dependencies, Maven will always check if there is a newer snapshot in the remote repository, and will download it in the local repository if this is the case.

The key here is to set up a continuous build so that the remote repository is constantly fed with the latest version of all the project's artifacts.

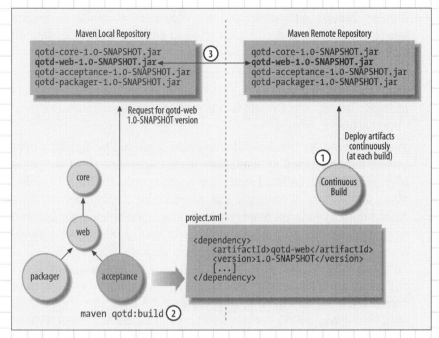

Figure 5-7. Building a Maven project using fresh binary dependencies

Let's take the example of the QOTD multiproject that you saw in Chapter 3, and let's imagine that you have added a new acceptance test to the acceptance subproject and you'd like to build it. In the previous lab you added a new qotd:deploy goal that deploys all the project's artifacts to the remote repository. You simply need to modify the maven. cruisecontrol.goals property that you used in the previous lab so that CruiseControl calls the qotd:deploy goal and thus deploys fresh artifacts whenever there's a code change:

```
maven.cruisecontrol.goals = scm:update|clean qotd:deploy
```

Now, simply type maven qotd:build:

```
C:\dev\mavenbook\code\qotd\acceptance>maven qotd:build
[...]
```

What just happened?

You have just set up one of the best possible Continuous Integration implementation strategies by using binary dependencies. Imagine the advantages of what you've set up:

- It's fast. Indeed, as a developer you only need to build the project you're working on and you don't need to perform an SCM update on all dependencies and rebuild them all.

- You're always using the latest versions of your project's dependencies, thus ensuring Continuous Integration. As soon as there's a code change, CruiseControl rebuilds the project and republishes the generated artifacts.

- Most importantly, it's fail-safe. Imagine that you're building your project dependencies by hand. You need to perform an SCM update to ensure you're building with the latest source modifications. But doing this is risky. If someone has introduced a change that causes a build failure, you'll get stuck when building the related project and you won't be able to proceed easily with your project's build. However, using this new binary dependency strategy you won't have to bear this: the `qotd:deploy` goal will deploy its artifacts only if the build has been successful, meaning that all artifacts in the remote repository are guaranteed to have passed the build! So, if one build fails, when you build your project it's going to use the latest dependencies that have successfully passed the build. Of course, this also means that the artifact qualities are only as good as your automated tests are! It really pays to invest in automated testing.

Writing Maven Plug-ins

You have seen that Maven is constructed from a series of plug-ins, and now it's time to build your own. You may want to do this for a few reasons:

Modularity
> Your project's *maven.xml* file is getting too big and you wish to streamline it.

Reusability
> You want to reuse the same build logic in several Maven projects.

Writing a Simple JAR Execution Plug-in

In this lab you'll write a plug-in which can run an executable JAR. This is a simple plug-in that should get you started with the basics of plug-in writing.

How do I do that?

The first thing to know is that a Maven plug-in is just another Maven project; any plug-in project will have the same structure as a normal Maven project: a *project.xml* file, a *project.properties* file, documentation in an *xdocs/* directory, etc. The only difference with a standard Maven project is that the *project.xml* file should not reference elements defined in a parent Project Object Model (POM). This is because the parent POM is not included when the plug-in is deployed and the referenced elements won't be found at execution time. Of course this doesn't matter if the reference elements are not used by the plug-in at runtime.

In addition to these standard Maven files, a plug-in project has two specific files, as shown in Figure 6-1:

plugin.jelly

This file defines a plug-in's goals, and it is where you will put all the plug-in logic in the form of Jelly script. This file resembles *maven.xml* as seen in previous chapters. While *plugin.jelly* and *maven.xml* contain similar goal definitions, they are separated to avoid conflicts: the *maven.xml* file is used at build time to build your plug-in, whereas *plugin.jelly* is used at runtime by users of your plug-in.

plugin.properties

This file defines default values for *plug-in properties*. A plug-in property is a property that end users of your plug-in can modify to suit their setup. The format of the *plugin.properties* file is the same as that of the *project.properties* file but, like *plugin.jelly*, *plugin. properties* is separated from *project.properties* (*project.properties* is used at build time to build your plug-in, whereas *plugin.properties* is used at runtime).

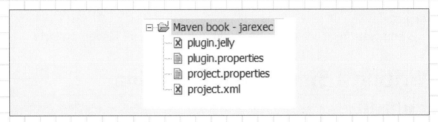

Figure 6-1. Minimal Maven plug-in structure

In order to run an executable JAR you simply need to use the Ant java task, using the jar attribute (see *http://ant.apache.org/manual/ CoreTasks/java.html* for the Ant Manual reference for the java task). Apply the plug-in's *plugin.jelly* file:

```
<?xml version="1.0"?>

<project
    xmlns:j="jelly:core"
    xmlns:ant="jelly:ant"
    xmlns:maven="jelly:maven">

  <goal name="jarexec:run" prereqs="jar:jar"
      description="Runs an executable JAR">

    <maven:get var="jarName" plugin="maven-jar-plugin"
        property="maven.jar.final.name"/>
```

```
    <ant:java jar="${maven.build.dir}/${jarName}" fork="true">
      <ant:classpath>
        <ant:path refid="maven.dependency.classpath"/>
      </ant:classpath>
    </ant:java>

  </goal>

</project>
```

_____

TIP

The maven.jar.final.name property was introduced in version 1.7
of the JAR plug-in, so be sure to use it. See   for directions on
installing a specific version of a plug-in.

_____

(margin note, handwritten) Document your plug-in's public goals by adding a description to them.

The jarexec:run goal depends on jar:jar and you've used the
description attribute to describe what the goal does. This is useful for
end users who can know the list of goals available in your plug-in by
typing maven -P jarexec.

One tricky part is getting the name of the JAR file that you wish to execute. As the user of this plug-in will have used the JAR plug-in to generate his JAR, you can ask the JAR plug-in for the JAR name using the
maven:get tag (see Chapter 2 for more details on maven:get). Then you
also need to add all the JARs defined as dependencies in the user's
project.xml file to the java task execution classpath. You do this by using
the predefined maven.dependency.classpath Maven property (internally
it is an Ant PATH element).

So far, you've not had to provide support for any property customizable by
the end user (your *plugin.properties* file is empty). Now you will add a
property that will allow an end user to change the name of the JAR to execute, and use a default name of maven.jar.final.name in case the user
does not modify it. It's good practice to always provide default values so
that your plug-in can work as is without modification from the user. It's
also good to provide possibilities for customization such as the ability to
override the name of the JAR to execute. Let's call mdn.jarexec.jar the
property for specifying which JAR to run. You could name it any way you
wish, but the accepted convention is to name it using this pattern:
[groupId].[plugin name].[some property name] (or just [plugin name].
[some property] if the groupId and the plug-in name are the same).

You might be tempted to write the following line in the *plugin.properties* file:

```
mdn.jarexec.jar = ${maven.jar.final.name}
```

You might be shocked to hear that this will not always work! This is because the `maven.jar.final.name` property is a property of the JAR plug-in, and Maven loads plug-in properties in memory the first time they are called (this is also known as lazy loading). This is done to isolate plug-in namespaces (see Chapter 2 for more details).

Thus, the preceding line of code will work only if the JAR plug-in has been called before the Jarexec plug-in itself is executed. Thankfully there's a solution! The solution is to retrieve the property from the JAR plug-in using the `maven:get` tag, as you did earlier. This tag loads the plug-in passed to it if it's not already loaded in memory, and then fetches the property.

Use the `maven:property` tag to set a default value to the `mdn.jarexec.jar` property, or use the value provided by the user (if defined):

```xml
<?xml version="1.0"?>

<project
    xmlns:j="jelly:core"
    xmlns:ant="jelly:ant"
    xmlns:maven="jelly:maven">

  <goal name="jarexec:run" depends="jar:jar">

    <maven:get var="defaultJarName" plugin="maven-jar-plugin"
        property="maven.jar.final.name"/>
    <j:set var="defaultJar" value="${maven.build.dir}/${defaultJarName}"/>
    <maven:property var="jar" name="mdn.jarexec.jar"
        defaultValue="${defaultJar}"/>

    <ant:java jar="${jar}" fork="true">
      <ant:classpath>
        <ant:path refid="maven.dependency.classpath"/>
      </ant:classpath>
    </ant:java>

  </goal>

</project>
```

What about...

...using the Javaapp plug-in?

There's an existing plug-in called Javaapp. It is used to generate a single JAR containing the project's Java classes and all classes from the project's dependencies. It has a `javaapp:run` goal, which runs an executable JAR.

Installing a Plug-in from Its Sources

Now that you know how to write a plug-in, let's install your newly created Jarexec plug-in in your local Maven installation.

How do I do that?

A plug-in is packaged as a JAR, so the first step is to configure the Jarexec project's build so that it generates a valid plug-in JAR. A valid plug-in JAR must contain some requisite files: *plugin.jelly*, *plugin.properties*, and (optionally) plug-in resources. Plug-in resources, as you will see in a following lab, are simply any file that is put in a *plugin-resources/* directory in the JAR.

You create a plug-in JAR by calling the `plugin:plugin` goal of the Plugin plug-in. In practice, this goal simply calls the `jar:jar` goal internally. To generate a valid JAR configure your *jarexec/project.xml* file and define a resources section to include *plugin.jelly*, *plugin.properties*, and any plug-in resources in your plug-in's JAR file:

```
<?xml version="1.0"?>

<project>
  <pomVersion>3</pomVersion>
  <artifactId>jarexec</artifactId>
  <name>JAR Executor</name>
  <groupId>mdn</groupId>
  [...]
  <build>
    <sourceDirectory>src/main</sourceDirectory>
    <unitTestSourceDirectory>src/test</unitTestSourceDirectory>

    <unitTest>
      <includes>
        <include>**/*Test.java</include>
      </includes>
    </unitTest>
```

```
<resources>
  <resource>
    <directory>src/plugin-resources</directory>
    <targetPath>plugin-resources</targetPath>
  </resource>
  <resource>
    <directory>.</directory>
    <includes>
      <include>plugin.jelly</include>
      <include>plugin.properties</include>
      <include>project.xml</include>
    </includes>
  </resource>
</resources>

    </build>

</project>
```

To build the plug-in and install it in your local Maven repository, run the plugin:install goal. Here is the output of this goal:

```
C:\dev\mavenbook\code\plugins\jarexec>maven plugin:install
[...]

plugin:plugin:
java:prepare-filesystem:

java:compile:
    [echo] Compiling to C:\dev\mavenbook\code\plugins\jarexec/target/classes
    [echo] No java source files to compile.

java:jar-resources:

test:prepare-filesystem:

test:test-resources:

test:compile:
    [echo] No test source files to compile.

test:test:
    [echo] No tests to run.

jar:jar:


plugin:install:
    [delete] Deleting 1 files from C:\apps\maven-1.0.2\plugins
    [delete] Deleting 4 files from C:\Documents and Settings\Vincent Massol\
.maven\cache
```

```
    [delete] Deleted 2 directories from C:\Documents and Settings\Vincent
Massol\.maven\cache
    [copy] Copying 1 file to C:\apps\maven-1.0.2\plugins
BUILD SUCCESSFUL
```

What just happened?

You just defined a plug-in's resources and installed a plug-in in your
local Maven installation. Chapter 2 showed you how to install a plug-in
from a remote repository, and this lab shows you how to install a plug-in
from a local source. You should now be able to download, customize, and
install any plug-in you may need to work with. The `plugin:install` goal
simply builds a plug-in and installs it in your local Maven installation. It
does this by copying your plug-in to *MAVEN_HOME/plugins*.

Maybe you're thinking about publishing your plug-in at this stage. Hold
on! You haven't tested it yet! Let's do that now; you'll discover how to
publish your plug-in at the end of this chapter.

Testing a Plug-in

If you're writing a plug-in for general consumption, it would be good if
you could ensure that it is working fine. You don't want to release something buggy, right? This lab will show you how to write automated tests
for your plug-in.

How do I do that?

You can write two types of tests: Java unit tests and functional tests.
Writing Java unit tests makes sense only if your plug-in is relying on
Java source code. You add JUnit tests to your plug-in project just as you
do for any Maven project: you add them to an *src/test* directory defined
using the `unitTestSourceDirectory` element in your *project.xml* file.
When you execute the `plugin:install` goal, your unit tests will run
automatically.

As most Maven plug-ins rely on Jelly script, it makes more sense to focus
on writing functional tests than it does to focus on JUnit tests. The Plugin
plug-in has a special `plugin:test` goal which automatically starts your
functional tests, provided you have put them in the *src/plugin-test* directory. A functional test is simply a Maven project that you put in *src/plugin-
test*. This Maven test project has to meet only one condition: it must have a
custom goal named `testPlugin` that you write in its *maven.xml* file. Under

the hood, this is the goal that will be called when you execute the plugin:test goal.

As you might need several functional tests for your plug-in, the best practice is to set up a Multiproject project in *src/plugin-test*. For example, for the Jarexec plug-in you might want to write a first test to verify that it can run a test JAR using the default JAR location (name this project *testDefaultJarExecution*) and a second test showing it can run a JAR that you specify using the mdn.jarexec.jar property (name this project *testJarExecutionWhenSpecifyingLocation*). The full directory structure will then be (see Figure 6-2):

src/plugin-test
> The location of the master Multiproject project.

src/plugin-test/testDefaultJarExecution
> The location of the functional test for testing default JAR execution. It also contains a Java class (Main.java) that is used to generate a test JAR.

src/plugin-test/testJarExecutionWhenSpecifyingLocation
> The location of the functional test for testing when the JAR location is specified using the mdn.jarexec.jar property. It also contains required Java sources for the test.

The *src/plugin-test/maven.xml* file contains a testPlugin goal that simply triggers the call of the testPlugin goals of all the subprojects, using the multiproject:goal goal (see Chapter 3 for a detailed introduction to the Multiproject project):

```
<project default="testPlugin" xmlns:j="jelly:core">

  <goal name="testPlugin">
    <j:set var="goal" value="testPlugin"/>
    <attainGoal name="multiproject:goal"/>
  </goal>

</project>
```

TIP

It's good practice to define a default testPlugin goal for test plug-ins (as shown earlier) so that when users type maven directly into their directories they will execute the tests.

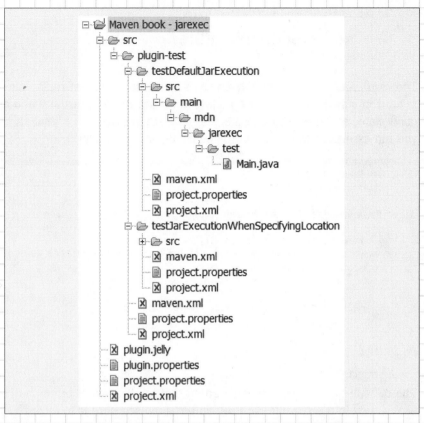

Figure 6-2. Jarexec project showing the functional test directory structure

The *src/plugin-test/project.xml* file is a standard POM defining all the elements common to all subprojects. Each subproject only needs to define what's different. For example, *src/plugin-test/testDefaultJarExecution/ project.xml* contains:

```xml
<?xml version="1.0"?>

<project>
  <extend>../project.xml</extend>
  <artifactId>jarexec-testDefaultJarExecution</artifactId>
  <name>jarexec-testDefaultJarExecution</name>
</project>
```

Have a look at the code for the `testDefaultJarExecution` project. The `Main.java` class is the simplest possible code for generating an executable JAR:

```java
package mdn.jarexec.test;

public class Main
{
```

```
        public static void main(String[] args)
        {
            System.out.println("It works...");
        }
    }
```

The *testDefaultJarExecution/maven.xml* file is where the test really happens. You start by cleaning the project to ensure that the test starts in a good state, and then you execute the jarexec:run goal. As a final step, you run assertions to verify that the outcome was successful:

```
<project default="testPlugin"
  xmlns:ant="jelly:ant"
  xmlns:assert="assert">

  <goal name="testPlugin" prereqs="clean">

    <ant:mkdir dir="${maven.build.dir}"/>
    <ant:record name="${maven.build.dir}/log.txt" action="start"/>
    <attainGoal name="jarexec:run"/>
    <ant:record name="${maven.build.dir}/log.txt" action="stop"/>

    <assert:assertFileContains file="${maven.build.dir}/log.txt"
        match="It works..."/>

  </goal>

</project>
```

The difficult part in this case is asserting that the Main class prints the It works… text in the console. One solution that is used here is to record the console output using the Ant record task and then use the assert tag library to verify that the recorded file contains the string you're looking for. The assert tag library is located in the Plugin plug-in. The assertFileContains tag is a new tag introduced in Version 1.6 of the Plugin plug-in. Make sure you have at least this version installed (see the Appendix for directions on installing a specific version of a plug-in).

TIP

In addition to exposing goals, plug-ins can also contribute tag libraries. This is the case for the Plugin plug-in, which offers an assert tag library. A Jelly script can define a new tag library using the Jelly define tag library (see *http://jakarta.apache.org/ commons/jelly/libs/define/tags.html* for reference documentation). To use a tag defined in another plug-in simply define its namespace as you did earlier for the assert tag library: xmlns: assert="assert".

Chapter 6: Writing Maven Plug-ins

Now you can run the plug-in test by executing the plugin:test goal:

```
C:\dev\mavenbook\code\plugins\jarexec>maven plugin:test
[...]
+-----------------------------------------
| Executing testPlugin jarexec-testDefaultJarExecution
| Memory: 3M/4M
+-----------------------------------------

multiproject:goal:
build:start:

testPlugin:
clean:clean:
    [delete] Deleting directory C:\dev\mavenbook\code\plugins\jarexec\src\
plugin-test\testDefaultJarExecution\target

clean:

    [mkdir] Created dir: C:\dev\mavenbook\code\plugins\jarexec\src\plugin-
test\testDefaultJarExecution\target
java:prepare-filesystem:
    [mkdir] Created dir: C:\dev\mavenbook\code\plugins\jarexec\src\plugin-
test\testDefaultJarExecution\target\classes

java:compile:
    [echo] Compiling to C:\dev\mavenbook\code\plugins\jarexec\src\plugin-
test\testDefaultJarExecution/target/classes
    [javac] Compiling 1 source file to C:\dev\mavenbook\code\plugins\
jarexec\src\plugin-test\testDefaultJarExecution\target\classes

java:jar-resources:

test:prepare-filesystem:
    [mkdir] Created dir: C:\dev\mavenbook\code\plugins\jarexec\src\plugin-
test\testDefaultJarExecution\target\test-classes
    [mkdir] Created dir: C:\dev\mavenbook\code\plugins\jarexec\src\plugin-
test\testDefaultJarExecution\target\test-reports

test:test-resources:

test:compile:
    [echo] No test source files to compile.

test:test:
    [echo] No tests to run.

jar:jar:
    [jar] Building jar: C:\dev\mavenbook\code\plugins\jarexec\src\plugin-
test\testDefaultJarExecution\target\jarexec-testDefaultJa
rExecution-1.0.jar
```

```
jarexec:run:
    [java] It works...

[...]
BUILD SUCCESSFUL
Total time: 11 seconds
```

What just happened?

You have learned how to automate testing for the plug-ins you write. You used the ant:record tag to record the output of the program's execution. ant:record takes the output of a program and saves it to a *log.txt* file which is then tested using the assert tag library. The assert tag library is used to see if *log.txt* contains the output expected from the execution of the test application.

What about...

...if I make a mistake while writing the plug-in and I get some cryptic error when running the plugin:test goal?

Yes, you have found one limitation of the Multiproject project: it does not provide perfect error reporting! It is possible to get the following cryptic error message:

```
BUILD FAILED
File...... C:\Documents and Settings\Vincent Massol\.maven\cache\maven-
plugin-plugin-1.6-SNAPSHOT\plugin.jelly
Element... maven:maven
Line...... 306
Column.... 34
Unable to obtain goal [testPlugin] -- C:\Documents and Settings\Vincent
Massol\.maven\cache\maven-multiproject-plugin-1.3.1\plugin
.jelly:217:9: <maven:reactor> Reactor subproject failure occurred
```

The solution is to ask Maven to generate a stack trace (maven plugin: test -e), as you learned in Chapter 1. Then the real error will appear in the stack trace. Another possibility is to go into your test project and type maven testPlugin (or simply maven if you have set the default goal to be testPlugin). Fix the problem and then try executing the tests again from the top level with the plugin:test goal.

Writing a Complex Plug-in: The Logifier

Now that you have written your first simple plug-in, try to write another plug-in, but this time you'll aim for something a bit more complex and useful. You are going to develop a plug-in that applies a Logging Aspect, which is defined using the AspectJ Aspect-Oriented Programming (AOP) implementation (*http://www.eclipse.org/aspectj/*) to any Maven project. This is a plug-in that will prove useful whenever you wish to automatically add debugging information to a Maven project's JAR. Once you've created this Logifier plug-in, you can modify it to do fancier Aspect-oriented magic, such as verifying that best practices are applied, writing a simple profiling tool, generating sequence diagrams automatically, benchmarking, etc.

How do I do that?

The user of the Logifier plug-in is any Maven project that generates a JAR and wishes to add logging statements around all public methods. You'll create a plug-in with the logifier:logify goal, which will apply a Logging Aspect to the project's Java *.class* files. The Logging Aspect will instrument the Maven project's Java *.class* files, adding debug calls around all public methods. The Logifier will generate a "logified" JAR containing this instrumented code, and whenever the "logified" JAR is executed, the debugging information added by the Logging Aspect will appear on the console. Figure 6-3 illustrates the Logifier plug-in and the process which you will use to "logify" a project's JAR file.

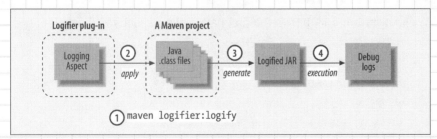

Figure 6-3. Architecture of the Logifier plug-in

To write the Logifier, you will need to complete the next few labs, which cover the following topics:

Developing a Logging Aspect

This is simple. You'll write a Logging Aspect using AspectJ. If you are new to Aspect-oriented programming, this will serve as a quick introduction. AOP is changing everything, from logging to EJBs, and now is your chance to learn.

Let's get started!

Packaging this Aspect in the Logifier plug-in

Once you've written the Aspect, you'll assemble all the pieces in a Maven plug-in.

Writing the Logifier plug-in's plugin.jelly file

This file performs the *weaving* (a nice word in Aspect terminology that means to apply an Aspect) of the Logging Aspect onto the target Java *.class* files and generates a "logified" JAR.

Executing the plug-in

Once you are finished, you'll install the plug-in and execute it to see the Logifier in action.

Writing a Logging Aspect Using AspectJ

The first thing to do is to write the Aspect you're going to apply to the project's code which will run the Logifier plug-in. The goal here is not to do a tutorial on AspectJ (for this, see *http://www.eclipse.org/aspectj/*).

How do I do that?

Without further ado, here's the first part of the Aspect you'll develop:

```
import org.aspectj.lang.reflect.*;
import org.aspectj.lang.*;

public aspect Logging
{
    /**
     * All public methods that have parameters.
     */
    pointcut publicMethodsWithParameterCalls() :
        !execution(public * *())
        && execution(public * *(..));

    /**
     * All public static methods that have parameters.
     */
```

```
    pointcut publicStaticMethodsWithParameterCalls() :
        !execution(public static * *())
        && execution(public static * *(..));
[...]
```

AspectJ extends the Java language and adds new keywords—among them aspect and pointcut. You can see here that the aspect keyword declares an Aspect (in lieu of the class keyword), and pointcut declares an identifier matching some code. AspectJ has a little language to express how to match portions of code. For example, the publicMethodsWithParameterCalls() PointCut Definition (PCD) translates to "whenever the code does not execute a public method with no parameter AND whenever the code executes a public method with parameters (signified by the .. notation, which means zero or more parameters)." Confused? In English, the previous logic-speak can be translated to: execution of all public methods that have parameters.

The next step is to tell the Logging Aspect what to do when the Point-Cuts are matched. You do this by using yet another new keyword, around():

```
    /**
     * Log all entries and exits of non-static methods that have no return
     * values.
     */
    Object around() :
        publicMethodsWithParameterCalls()
        && !publicStaticMethodsWithParameterCalls()
    {
        // Log the entry
        System.out.println('<' + getFullSignature(thisJoinPoint));

        long t1 = System.currentTimeMillis();

        // Execute the method
        final Object result = proceed();

        long t2 = System.currentTimeMillis();

        // Log the exit
        String output = '>' + thisJoinPoint.getSignature().getName();
        if (result != null)
        {
            output = output + " = [" + result + ']';
        }
        System.out.println(output + " (" + (t2-t1) + "ms)");

        return result;
    }
[...]
```

The `around` keyword is called *advice* in AspectJ terminology, and it tells the Aspect what to do when a PCD is matched. There are three main types of advice: `before( )`, `after( )`, and `around( )`. `before( )` is executed before the matching PCD, `after( )` is executed after the matching PCD, and `around( )` is executed around your PCD. In the `around( )` advice used earlier, `proceed( )` is used to execute the method matched by the PCD, and to capture the method's return value.

So, here you're saying "run this piece of code whenever you find execution of public methods with parameters that are not static methods." Why do you want this? This is just an example, and in practice we've found that logging methods with no parameters generates too many logs and is not too useful. In this example, static methods are excluded because the special `thisJoinPoint` variable does not exist for static methods, and to address static methods you would need to write this advice differently (look at the source code for the full example containing support for static calls).

The rest of the code is standard Java code that prints the signature of the wrapped method using `getFullSignature( )`. If you are interested in seeing the output generated by `getFullSignature( )`, take a look at the same source code on *http://www.mavenbook.org*. As a little bonus, the previous code also computes the time it has taken to execute the wrapped method, thus playing the role of a very lightweight profiling tool.

So, now that you've created a simple Aspect, combine this with your knowledge of Maven plug-ins and create a plug-in to apply this Aspect to any Maven project.

Using Plug-in Resources

The Logifier plug-in requires that the Logging Aspect file be bundled in the plug-in JAR so that, at runtime, it can weave the Logging Aspect onto the target project's code.

How do I do that?

There's a special place for plug-in resources in a plug-in project: *src/ plugin-resources*. Figure 6-4 shows the Logifier plug-in file structure showing the Aspect saved in a *Logging.aj* file.

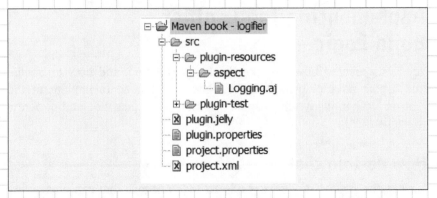

Figure 6-4. Logifier plug-in's file structure showing the Logging.aj plug-in resource

Tell Maven to copy these resources in the generated plug-in JAR. You do this by using the resource element in the plug-in's *project.xml* file:

```
<build>
[...]

  <resources>
    <resource>
      <directory>src/plugin-resources</directory>
      <targetPath>plugin-resources</targetPath>
    </resource>
    <resource>
      <directory>.</directory>
      <includes>
        <include>plugin.jelly</include>
        <include>plugin.properties</include>
        <include>project.xml</include>
      </includes>
    </resource>
  </resources>
</build>
```

This means that your *Logging.aj* file will be located in a *plugin-resources/aspect* directory inside the generated plug-in JAR.

Now you can reference any resource from your *plugin.jelly* file, or in the *plugin.properties* file using the ${plugin.resources} expression. For example, to reference the *Logging.aj* Aspect you'd write ${plugin.resources}/aspect/Logging.aj. You'll see how this is used in the next section.

Implementing the Logifier
Build Logic

You've discovered how to write the Logging Aspect and how to bundle this Aspect as a plug-in resource. Now, you'll need to implement the plug-in logic to weave the Aspect into the Java *.class* files and generate a "logified" JAR.

How do I do that?

Luckily, the AspectJ framework has an `iajc` Ant task that can weave any Aspect onto a set of Java source files, JAR files, or Java bytecode (*.class* files).

In this plug-in, you'll weave the Logging Aspect onto *.class* files. Here's the part of your *plugin.jelly* file that weaves the Aspect and generates the logified JAR:

```xml
<?xml version="1.0"?>

<project
    xmlns:j="jelly:core"
    xmlns:ant="jelly:ant"
    xmlns:maven="jelly:maven">

  <goal name="logifier:compile" prereqs="java:compile">

    <ant:iajc destDir="${maven.build.dest}">
      <ant:sourceroots>
        <ant:pathelement location="${plugin.resources}/aspect"/>
      </ant:sourceroots>
      <ant:inpath>
        <ant:pathelement location="${maven.build.dest}"/>
      </ant:inpath>
      <ant:classpath>
        <ant:path refid="maven.dependency.classpath"/>
        <ant:pathelement
            path="${plugin.getDependencyPath('aspectj:aspectjrt')}"/>
      </ant:classpath>
    </ant:iajc>

  </goal>

  <goal name="logifier:logify" prereqs="logifier:compile,jar"
        description="Generate a logified JAR"/>

</project>
```

You have created two goals: `logifier:compile` and `logifier:logify`. The `logifier:compile` goal calls `java:compile` to compile the Java source files into *.class* files, and the `iajc` Ant task weaves the Aspect onto these *.class* files. The `logifier:logify` goal is in charge of generating the "logified" JAR: it does this very simply by calling the JAR plug-in.

The `iajc` Ant task is an Ant task that you can find in the AspectJ *aspectjtools.jar* JAR, located in AspectJ's distribution. The `destDir` attribute specifies where the weaved *.class* files will be output. Note that you are overwriting the existing *.class* files generated by `java:compile`. That makes it simpler to reuse the JAR plug-in afterward (you don't have to tell it to look for *.class* files in a location different from its default).

You specify the location of your Aspect definitions using the `sourceroots` Ant `PATH` element, and you specify the source *.class* files to weave onto using the `inpath` PATH element.

Now here's something interesting—referencing a dependency defined in *project.xml* from within your *project.jelly* file. You do this using the getDependencyPath( ) method on the `plugin` object (this is a Java object representing the plug-in POM), passing to it a string with the format groupId:artifactId. Here you're referencing the `aspectj:aspectjrt` artifact which needs to be defined in the plug-in's *project.xml* as follows (1.2.1 is the latest version at the time of this writing):

```
<dependencies>
  <dependency>
    <groupId>aspectj</groupId>
    <artifactId>aspectjrt</artifactId>
    <version>1.2.1</version>
  </dependency>
```

This *aspectjrt.jar* JAR is required for weaving by the `iajc` task.

But, hey, hold on! There is something missing. Where have you defined the `iajc` Ant task? It's not part of the standard Ant distribution (the one

bundled with Maven), and thus you need to introduce it via the `taskdef`
Ant task, as you would for any custom Ant task! To successfully define
this task, you will also need to add the *aspectjtools.jar* JAR to the classpath, as the `iajc` task depends on it. Refactor the *plugin.jelly* file to add a
`logifier:init` goal to `taskdef` the `iajc` task as follows:

```
<?xml version="1.0"?>

<project
    xmlns:j="jelly:core"
    xmlns:ant="jelly:ant"
    xmlns:maven="jelly:maven">

  <goal name="logifier:init">

    <ant:taskdef
        resource="org/aspectj/tools/ant/taskdefs/aspectjTaskdefs.properties">
      <ant:classpath>
        <ant:pathelement
            path="${plugin.getDependencyPath('aspectj:aspectjtools')}"/>
      </ant:classpath>
    </ant:taskdef>

  </goal>

  <goal name="logifier:compile" prereqs="logifier:init,java:compile">

    <ant:iajc destDir="${maven.build.dest}">
    [...]
```

You'll need to add a reference to the *aspectjtools* artifact in your *project.
xml* file, and by now you should be familiar with the steps involved in
adding dependencies. Here's the new dependency from *project.xml*:

```
<dependencies>
  <dependency>
    <groupId>aspectj</groupId>
    <artifactId>aspectjrt</artifactId>
    <version>1.2.1</version>
  </dependency>
  <dependency>
    <groupId>aspectj</groupId>
    <artifactId>aspectjtools</artifactId>
    <version>1.2.1</version>
  </dependency>
</dependencies>
```

You are almost there. One little detail remains... Remember this *aspectjrt*
JAR? Well, as its name implies (rt stands for runtime) it is required to be
in the classpath when executing the "logified" JAR. Yuck! That's not cool,

as any Maven project that wants to use your "logified" plug-in will also need to add the *aspectjrt* JAR to its dependency list... But there's a solution! Why not bundle the *aspectjrt* JAR into the "logified" JAR? This would work, except in the very unlikely case where the Maven project is already using a different version of AspectJ than the version used by the Logifier. But, if that were the case, you wouldn't need to bundle *aspectjrt* JAR at all!

You can easily add the *aspectjrt* class files to your JAR file by adding the following ant:jar task to update the contents of your project's JAR artifact. Executing the jar task in update mode adds the contents of the *aspectjrt* JAR:

Simple, isn't it?

```
<goal name="logifier:logify" prereqs="logifier:compile,jar"
    description="Generate a logified JAR">

  <maven:get var="jarName" plugin="maven-jar-plugin"
      property="maven.jar.final.name"/>
  <j:set var="jar" value="${maven.build.dir}/${jarName}"/>

  <ant:jar destfile="${jar}" update="true">
    <ant:zipfileset
        src="${plugin.getDependencyPath('aspectj:aspectjrt')}"/>
  </ant:jar>

</goal>
```

Executing the Logifier Plug-in

At this point you must be anxious to see the Logifier plug-in executing... As you are a good developer, your first instinct is to write tests for the plug-in which will also serve as an execution bed. Good call!

How do I do that?

You already saw in a previous lab how to write a plug-in test, so focus on the parts specific to the Logifier plug-in. Figure 6-5 show the typical test directory structure.

The *testLogifierExecution* subproject is a Maven project that has some source (*Main.java*) and which generates an executable JAR (the *project. properties* file defines the maven.jar.mainclass property to specify the main class: maven.jar.mainclass = mdn.logifier.test.Main).

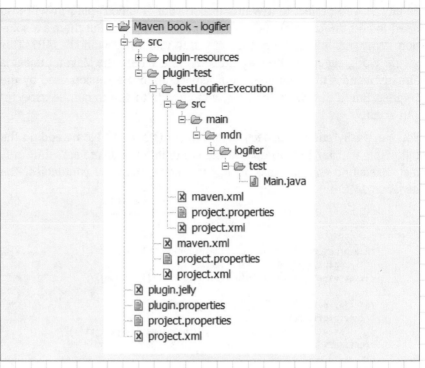

Figure 6-5. Logifier plug-in directory structure showing the plug-in tests

The Main.java class contains some very simple code meant to trigger the Logging Aspect:

```java
package mdn.logifier.test;

public class Main
{
    public static void main(String[ ] args)
    {
        Main main = new Main( );
        main.display1("It works1...");
        main.display2("It works2...");
    } .

    public void display1(String message)
    {
        System.out.println(message);
    }

    public int display2(String message)
    {
        System.out.println(message);
        return 1;
    }
}
```

The *maven.xml* file is very similar in content to the one you saw in the "Testing a Plug-in" lab earlier in this chapter, and it verifies that the Logging Aspect has executed by asserting the content of the console output:

```
<project default="testPlugin"
  xmlns:ant="jelly:ant"
  xmlns:assert="assert">

  <goal name="testPlugin" prereqs="clean">

    <attainGoal name="logifier:logify"/>

    <ant:record name="${maven.build.dir}/log.txt" action="start"/>
    <attainGoal name="jarexec:run"/>
    <ant:record name="${maven.build.dir}/log.txt" action="stop"/>

    <assert:assertFileContains file="${maven.build.dir}/log.txt"
        match="display1([It works1...])"/>
    <assert:assertFileContains file="${maven.build.dir}/log.txt"
        match="display2([It works2...])"/>

  </goal>

</project>
```

Notice that you have cleverly reused the Jarexec plug-in that you created in the first lab. Execute it by building the plug-in (maven plugin:install) and running the test (maven plugin:test):

```
C:\dev\mavenbook\code\plugins\logifier>maven plugin:test
[...]

logifier:init:

java:prepare-filesystem:
    [mkdir] Created dir: C:\dev\mavenbook\code\plugins\logifier\src\plugin-
test\testLogifierExecution\target\classes

java:compile:
    [echo] Compiling to C:\dev\mavenbook\code\plugins\logifier\src\plugin-
test\testLogifierExecution/target/classes
    [javac] Compiling 1 source file to C:\dev\mavenbook\code\plugins\
logifier\src\plugin-test\testLogifierExecution\target\classes

logifier:compile:

[...]

jar:jar:
    [jar] Building jar: C:\dev\mavenbook\code\plugins\logifier\src\plugin-
test\testLogifierExecution\target\logifier-testLogifierExecution-1.0.jar

jar:

logifier:logify:
```

```
        [jar] Updating jar: C:\dev\mavenbook\code\plugins\logifier\src\plugin-
    test\testLogifierExecution\target\logifier-testLogifierE
    xecution-1.0.jar

    [...]

jarexec:run:
    [java] <display1([It works1...])
    [java] It works1...
    [java] >display1 (0ms)
    [java] <display2([It works2...])
    [java] It works2...
    [java] >display2 = [1] (0ms)
BUILD SUCCESSFUL
Total time: 5 seconds
```

Wow! You're done. And it works!

Adding Dynamic Dependencies

Maven dependency handling supports only static dependencies defined in *project.xml*. However, there are times when a plug-in will need to add a dependency at runtime.

How do I do that?

Consider your favorite plug-in—Logifier. The way you wrote it in the previous lab has a severe limitation. Imagine that you're running it on a Maven project that has unit tests. As you know, running the `jar` goal will automatically execute the `test:test` goal and run the unit tests. As your `logifier:logify` goal depends on the `jar` goal, it'll end up running the unit tests on the "logified" code... Yikes! This means that the test will fail, with this error:

```
java.lang.NoClassDefFoundError: org/aspectj/lang/Signature
```

Not only is this error message unexpected to someone not familiar with the Logifier plug-in, but also you have a plug-in causing problems in an unrelated plug-in—test. In order to fix this, you need to rewrite the JAR plug-in so that it doesn't execute tests, or tell it to skip the tests. Or better yet, add the *aspectjrt* JAR to the classpath at runtime. This sounds like the best solution.

You can add a dependency dynamically by using the `addPath` tag provided by Maven:

```
    <goal name="logifier:init">
[...]
        <ant:path id="aspectjrt.classpath">
```

```
        <ant:pathelement
            path="${plugin.getDependencyPath('aspectj:aspectjrt')}"/>
    </ant:path>
    <maven:addPath id="maven.dependency.classpath"
        refid="aspectjrt.classpath"/>

</goal>
```

When your project executes, the `logifier:init` goal will be called and the *aspectjrt* artifact will be added to the `maven.dependency.classpath` before any other goals are executed. You can see in the goal definition that you are using `${plugin.getDependencyPath('aspectj:aspectjrt')}` to retrieve the path to this JAR file, and then you are adding it to the classpath with the `maven:addPath` tag which takes the `id` of the path to alter and the `refid` of the path to add.

What just happened?

You have taken the first version of the Logifier plug-in and transformed it into a more intelligent plug-in that now supports generating debug logs when the project unit tests are executed. You did this by making the runtime AspectJ dependency a dynamic dependency added during the initialization of the Logifier plug-in. Now you are ready to tackle the next challenge of the Logifier plug-in: adding a report to the project web site.

Writing a Plug-in That Generates Reports

Throughout this book you have used several Maven plug-ins that generate reports when you type `maven site` (Checkstyle, Dashboard, JUnit, etc.). Wouldn't it be nice if you could add your own report type that users of your plug-in could add to their `reports` section in the POM? In this lab you'll add a report that displays the logs generated by the Logging Aspect of your Logifier plug-in.

How do I do that?

Any plug-in can generate a report. All you need to do is define three goals in your plug-in's *plugin.jelly* file. Assuming you want to name the report `maven-logifier-plugin`, these goals are:

- `maven-logifier-plugin:register`
- `maven-logifier-plugin:deregister`
- `maven-logifier-plugin:report`

Have a look at how to implement the `maven-logifier-plugin:register` goal:

```
<?xml version="1.0"?>

<project
    xmlns:j="jelly:core"
    xmlns:ant="jelly:ant"
    xmlns:maven="jelly:maven"
    xmlns:doc="doc">
  [...]
    <goal name="maven-logifier-plugin:register">
    <doc:registerReport
        name="Logifier"
        pluginName="maven-logifier-plugin"
        description=
            "Report showing all debugging logs generated by the Logging
            Aspect" link="logifier-report"/>
    </goal>
```

You need to understand how the `maven-logifier-plugin:register` goal fits in the report generation lifecycle. It is called by the XDoc plug-in when the user types `maven site` (as you'll recall, the XDoc plug-in is used by the Site plug-in). The XDoc plug-in gets the list of reports defined in the `reports` section of the POM (as seen in Chapter 1) and calls the `[report name]:register` goal for each report found. Inside this goal you need to use the `doc:registerReport` tag provided by the XDoc plug-in to register your report. This registration provides information to the XDoc plug-in so that it can generate a menu entry for each report in the navigation menu. A typical `reports` section of the navigation menu is shown in Figure 6-6.

The attributes for `doc:registerReport` provide the following information:

name

> The name that appears in the navigation menu in Figure 6-6.

pluginName

> The internal plug-in name that the XDoc plug-in uses to store your registration information. You can use any name you want. However, as you'll see later on, this name will be used by the Site plug-in to compute the goal to call for generating the report.

description

> The report descriptions that appears in Figure 6-6 in the table of the Overview section.

link

> The report file name that is called when the user clicks the report link, excluding the HTML extension.

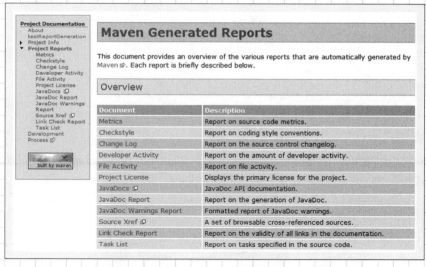

Figure 6-6. reports section showing all registered reports

The `maven-logifier-plugin:deregister` goal is even simpler:

```
<goal name="maven-logifier-plugin:deregister">
  <doc:deregisterReport name="maven-logifier-plugin"/>
</goal>
```

In practice this goal is not called by the Site plug-in. A Maven project using your plug-in would call it if it wanted to remove your report from the list of registered reports.

The last goal to implement is `maven-logifier-plugin:report`. This goal is called automatically by the Site plug-in when it generates the web site. It computes the goal name by getting the `pluginName` attribute that you used in the `doc:registerReport` tag, using the `[pluginName]:report` formula.

You want your report to integrate with the look-and-feel of the Maven web site, so you're going to generate a report in the standard XDoc format (see Chapter 2) used for project documentation. Before you can do that, you need to output Logifier's debug logs in XML so that they can be easily transformed to the XDoc format using the Jelly Scripting Language (JSL).

Modifying the *Logging.aj* Aspect to output an XML file instead of `System.out` logs is outside the scope of this lab. If you are interested in seeing how the Logifier has been altered to output XML, check the source code at *http://www.mavenbook.org* for more information. For the purposes of this lab, all you need to know is the format of the logging output generated by the modified *Logging.aj* Aspect:

```
<logs>
  <log type="entry" call="name of method called and parameters"/>
  <log type="exit" call="name of method called" time="method response time"
    return="return value (only if there is one)"/>
  [...]
</logs>
```

It's time to learn how to use JSL.

What just happened?

You are slowly transforming the first version of the Logifier to support report generation using the workflow defined in Figure 6-7.

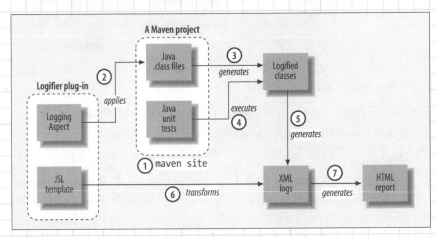

Figure 6-7. The new Logifier's workflow for producing an HTML report

The process in the new Logifier is defined as follows:

1. The user executes the site goal to generate the project's web site after having added the maven-logifier-plugin report to the reports section of its POM.

2. The Site plug-in calls the maven-logifier-plugin:report goal, which in turn calls the logifier:logify goal. The first action of this goal is to apply the Logging Aspect on the project's Java *.class* files.

3. The Logging Aspect generates "logified" *.class* files.

4. The logifier:logify goal calls the jar goal which automatically executes the test:test goal, executing the Java unit tests on the "logified" classes.

5. As the "logified" classes are instrumented, they generate XML logs to be used in the subsequent report generation.

6. The `maven-logifier-plugin` goal now performs a JSL transformation on the XML log, which generates an XDoc file.

7. The Site plug-in transforms all the XDoc *.xml* files that have been generated by all registered reports into HTML (using Maven's CSS).

You have reached step 5 so far: the Logifier has gone from a plug-in that applies an Aspect, to a plug-in with a dynamic dependency, to a plug-in which generates an XML file used in the creation of a report. This is no longer just a simple plug-in. You are learning how to create some of the most advanced plug-ins available. And you thought this was going to be a simple introduction to Maven. While this book is a simple introduction to Maven, you should be convinced by now that Maven plug-ins are accessible and easy to create.

The next lab will take you through the process of transforming an XML file to XDoc via JSL, an XSLT-like language with the ability to reuse Jelly and Ant tags.

Creating an XDoc File Using JSL

This lab continues with the Logifier plug-in by adding a `maven-logifier-plugin:report` goal that transforms the XML debug log generated by the `logifier:logify` goal into XDoc format. You will use JSL and the XDoc plug-in to perform this magical feat.

How do I do that?

The XDoc plug-in provides a `jsl` tag that you can use to apply a JSL transformation on an XML file. The following report generation goal uses this `jsl` tag to transform the Logifier log file to XDoc:

```
<goal name="maven-logifier-plugin:report" prereqs="logifier:logify">
  <doc:jsl
      input="${mdn.logifier.logfile}"
      output="logifier-report.xml"
      stylesheet="${plugin.resources}/template/logifier.jsl"
      outputMode="xml"/>
</goal>
```

The input attribute points to the XML file you wish to transform—in this case the log file generated by Logifier. As an experienced plug-in writer, you've created a new `mdn.logifier.logfile` property which points to the location where the Logging Aspect has generated its XML logs. Logifier defines a default value for `mdn.logifier.logfile` in *plugin.properties* as follows:

```
mdn.logifier.logfile = ${maven.build.dir}/logifier.xml
```

The output attribute is the XDoc file that will be generated by the JSL transformation. Notice that you have used a filename (*logifier-report.xml*) that matches the link attribute used earlier in the maven-logifier-plugin:register goal:

```
<doc:registerReport
  name="Logifier"
  pluginName="maven-logifier-plugin"
  description=
      "Report showing all debugging logs generated by the Logging Aspect"
  link="logifier-report"/>
```

The stylesheet attribute points to the JSL file that you'll write in just a second, and outputMode tells the tag that we're outputting XML.

Declarative XSLT purists beware. JSL is the best of both worlds.

What about this JSL? Isn't it just like XSLT? Why not just use XSLT? Those familiar with XSLT will find it similar to JSL. The major difference is that a JSL file can use any of the existing Jelly or Ant tags. While XSLT supports only a declarative programming model, JSL allows you to perform the same transformations using imperative programming models. In other words, while XSLT is a popular language for XML transformations, its basis in functional programming makes it difficult (if not impossible) to perform the simplest of tasks. JSL gives you the same feature set of XSLT, plus the ability to execute any Jelly tag. In addition, all Maven variables are available directly from within the JSL file.

Call the JSL file *logifier.jsl*, and put it in the *plugin-resources* directory in *src/plugin-resources/template/logifier.jsl*:

```
<?xml version="1.0"?>

<jsl:stylesheet
  select="$doc"
  xmlns:jsl="jelly:jsl"
  xmlns:x="jelly:xml"
  xmlns="logifier" trim="false">

<jsl:template match="logs">
  <document>
    <properties>
      <title>Logifier Report</title>
    </properties>
    <body>
      <section name="Logifier report">
        <table>
          <tr>
            <th>Type</th>
            <th>Call</th>
            <th>Return value</th>
            <th>Performance (ms)</th>
          </tr>
```

```
                <jsl:applyTemplates/>
            </table>
         </section>
      </body>
   </document>
</jsl:template>

<jsl:template match="log">
   <tr>
      <td><x:expr select="@type"/></td>
      <td><x:expr select="@call"/></td>
      <td><x:expr select="@return"/></td>
      <td><x:expr select="@time"/></td>
   </tr>
</jsl:template>

</jsl:stylesheet>
```

You could consider an XDoc file to be a styleless HTML file. XDoc does encompass a few special tags, such as the main document tag (equivalent to the HTML tag) and the section tag, which will be rendered as a page section. The title tag is nested within a properties tag. You can find more information about the XDoc format in Chapter 2.

JSL is going to remind you of XSLT because it fills the same role as XSLT. The JSL document is declared using the jsl:stylesheet tag. The doc variable represents the parsed XML document. The jsl:template nested content is executed whenever the XML document matches the match attribute. Thus, the jsl:template match="log" snippet is going to be called every time there is a log entry in the XML file. For example, for the following XML file it will be called four times:

```
<logs>
   <log type="entry" call="display1([testDisplay1])"/>
   <log type="exit" call="display1" time="0"/>
   <log type="entry" call="display2([testDisplay2])"/>
   <log type="exit" call="display2" return="1" time="0"/>
</logs>
```

The x:expr tag uses an XPath expression relative to the current XML node. Thus, x:expr select="@type" selects the type attribute of the log element. Quite simply, you are creating an HTML table which contains four columns that correspond to the information contained in the Logifier log file. These four columns are printed out in the jsl:template matching the log element.

The last step is to modify the *testLogifierExecution* test project that you created in the "Executing the Logifier Plug-in" lab earlier in this chapter. Start by renaming it to *testReportGeneration* and modify its *project.xml* file to add the Logifier report to the reports section:

```xml
<?xml version="1.0"?>

<project>
  <extend>../project.xml</extend>
  <artifactId>logifier-testReportGeneration</artifactId>
  <name>logifier-testReportGeneration</name>
  <reports>
    <report>maven-logifier-plugin</report>
  </reports>
</project>
```

Modify the *maven.xml* file to trigger report generation using the site goal:

```xml
<project default="testPlugin" xmlns:assert="assert">

  <goal name="testPlugin" prereqs="clean">
    <attainGoal name="site"/>
    <assert:assertFileExists file="${maven.docs.dest}/logifier-report.html"/>
  </goal>

</project>
```

Now you need to create a unit test that will trigger the test application. The new Logifier's directory structure is shown in Figure 6-8.

Rename the Main.java class to Display.java (you don't need a main( ) method anymore, now that you're triggering the Logifier by using unit tests instead of using an executable JAR):

```java
package mdn.logifier.test;

public class Display
{
    public void display1(String message)
    {
        System.out.println(message);
    }

    public int display2(String message)
    {
        System.out.println(message);
        return 1;
    }
}
```

And here's the associated DisplayTest containing the unit tests:

```java
package mdn.logifier.test;

import junit.framework.TestCase;

public class DisplayTest extends TestCase
{
    public void testDisplay1()
    {
```

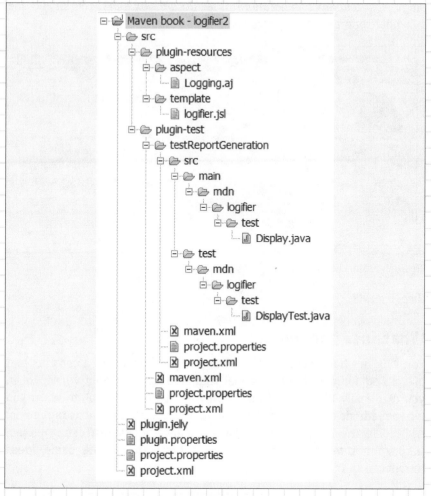

Figure 6-8. Directory structure for the new Logifier

```
        Display display = new Display();
        display.display1("testDisplay1");
    }

    public void testDisplay2()
    {
        Display display = new Display();
        assertEquals(1, display.display2("testDisplay2"));
    }
}
```

Now is the time to sit back and reap the fruits of your hard labor! Run the plugin:test goal and enjoy. The build should be successful, and you should be able to open the generated web site (located in *logifier/src/*

plugin-test/testReportGeneration/target/docs/index.html). You should see a Logifier report in the reports section (see Figure 6-9).

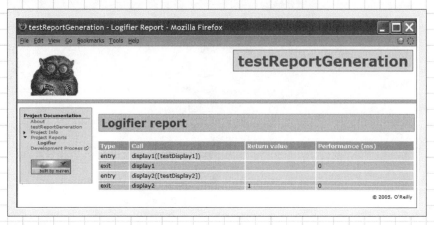

Figure 6-9. The Logifier report

Nice, isn't it?

What just happened?

You may not have realized it yet, but you just developed a complex and useful Logifier plug-in. Well done! Although this is a first version of it, you can easily modify it to be a lightweight profiling tool, to warn you when methods take too long to execute, to understand an existing project by tracing the execution flow, etc. Actually, the PatternTesting project (*http://patterntesting.sourceforge.net*) is built around the same ideas introduced in this chapter.

TIP

Here's a tip that may save you a number of frustrating hours: install the source code for all Maven plug-ins on your hard drive and create a project in your IDE for them. Then, whenever you don't know how to implement something, do a search on the existing plug-in. You can be sure one of them has it implemented!

You can get the Maven plug-in sources by using a Subversion client and checking them out from *http://svn.apache.org/repos/asf/maven/maven-1/plugins/trunk*, or you can point directly to your Maven *~userhome/.maven/cache* directory where all your installed plug-ins are expanded.

Publishing a Plug-in to a Remote Repository

As a plug-in writer, the last step of your journey is to learn how to share your plug-ins with others. To make your Logifier plug-in available to other developers, publish your plug-in to a remote Maven repository.

How do I do that?

The Plugin plug-in has a `plugin:repository-deploy` goal that you can use to deploy your plug-in to a remote Maven repository. This goal is equivalent to the `jar:deploy` and `war:deploy` goals that you saw in Chapter 4. Configure the deployment properties as described in Chapter 4. For example, using SCP:

```
maven.repo.list = mavenbook

maven.repo.mavenbook = scp://www.mavenbook.org
maven.repo.mavenbook.directory = /var/www/html/maven

maven.repo.mavenbook.username = vmassol
maven.repo.mavenbook.password = somepassword
```

Now deploy the plug-in to the remote repository:

```
C:\dev\mavenbook\code\plugins\logifier2>maven plugin:repository-deploy
[...]

plugin:repository-deploy:
    [echo] maven.repo.list is set - using artifact deploy mode
Will deploy to 1 repository(ies): mavenbook
Deploying to repository: mavenbook
Deploying: C:\dev\mavenbook\code\plugins\logifier2\project.xml-->mdn/poms/
logifier-1.0.pom
Executing command: mkdir -p /var/www/html/maven/mdn/poms

Executing command: chmod g+w /var/www/html/maven/mdn/poms/logifier-1.0.pom

Deploying: C:\dev\mavenbook\code\plugins\logifier2\project.xml.md5-->mdn/
poms/logifier-1.0.pom.md5
Executing command: mkdir -p /var/www/html/maven/mdn/poms

Executing command: chmod g+w /var/www/html/maven/mdn/poms/logifier-1.0.pom.
md5

Will deploy to 1 repository(ies): mavenbook
Deploying to repository: mavenbook
Deploying: C:\dev\mavenbook\code\plugins\logifier2\target\maven\logifier-1.
0.jar-->mdn/plugins/logifier-1.0.jar
Executing command: mkdir -p /var/www/html/maven/mdn/plugins
```

```
Executing command: chmod g+w /var/www/html/maven/mdn/plugins/logifier-1.0.
jar

Deploying: C:\dev\mavenbook\code\plugins\logifier2\target\maven\logifier-1.
0.jar.md5-->mdn/plugins/logifier-1.0.jar.md5
Executing command: mkdir -p /var/www/html/maven/mdn/plugins

Executing command: chmod g+w /var/www/html/maven/mdn/plugins/logifier-1.0.
jar.md5

BUILD SUCCESSFUL
```

What just happened?

Congratulations, you are now a plug-in developer. Enjoy Maven!

Maven Plug-ins

Plug-ins Reference

The following table lists all the Maven plug-ins that we covered in this book, and the chapters containing labs describing how to use them. In order to follow the labs you'll need to ensure that you have the plug-in versions mentioned in the table. Most of the time the labs will also work if your plug-in versions are greater than the ones mentioned, and may work if you have another version, although that is not guaranteed. Type maven -i in a command shell to check the versions of your installed plug-ins.

For your convenience the table also mentions in the third column whether the plug-in version mentioned is distributed in the Maven 1.0.2 release (the one that was available at the time of this writing). Thus, if you're using Maven 1.0.2 you should only install plug-ins that have an "N" in this column. If you're using Maven 1.1 or greater, you'll only need to install the plug-ins that are not part of the Maven distribution. They are:

- The Axis plug-in
- The Findbugs plug-in

If you need to install a new plug-in version, there are three ways you can make it available to a Maven project:

- By installing it in your local Maven installation using the Plugin plug-in
- By installing it manually in your local Maven installation
- By adding a dependency to the plug-in in your project's Project Object Model (POM)

These three methods are described later in this appendix. Table A-1 gives more information about plug-ins.

Table A-1. Plug-ins

Plug-in name	Minimal plug-in version	In Maven 1.0.2?	Covered in chapter(s)
Announcement	1.3	Y	4
Ant	1.8.1	Y	1
Artifact	1.4.1	Y	4
Axis	0.7	N	2
Changelog	1.8	N	4
Changes	1.5.1	Y	4
Checkstyle	2.5	Y	4
Clover	1.8	Y	4
Console	1.1	Y	1
CruiseControl	1.7	N	5
Dashboard	1.8	N	4
Developer-Activity	1.5.1	Y	4
Eclipse	1.9	Y	1
FAQ	1.4	Y	2
File-Activity	1.5.1	Y	4
Findbugs	0.8.4	N	4
Genapp	2.2	Y	1
JAR	1.7	N	1, 6
Java	1.5	Y	1
JavaDoc	1.7	Y	1
Jetty	1.1	Y	3
Multiproject	1.4	N	3, 4
Plugin	1.6	N	2, 6
PMD	1.6	Y	4
SCM	1.5	N	5
Site	1.5.2	Y	1, 4
StatCVS-XML	2.6	Y	4
Test	1.6.2	Y	1, 3
War	1.6.1	Y	3
XDoc	1.8	Y	2, 4, 6

You can obtain reference documentation about the Maven plug-ins at:

- *http://maven.apache.org/reference/plugins/index.html* for all plug-ins included in the Maven distribution
- *http://maven-plugins.sourceforge.net/* for plug-ins provided by the Maven-Plugins SourceForge project (Findbugs, Javaapp, etc.)

- *http://maven.apache.org/reference/3rdparty.html* for other third-party plug-ins

Auto-Downloading a Plug-in

Maven has a Plugin plug-in that allows you to download and install plug-ins from one or several Maven remote repositories. To use it, type the following on a single line:

```
maven plugin:download
  -DgroupId=[plug-in group id]
  -DartifactId=[plug-in artifact id]
  -Dversion=[plug-in version]
```

where:

- [plug-in group id] is the plug-in's groupId. For all plug-ins provided by Maven, that's maven.
- [plug-in artifact id] is the plug-in's artifactId. For example, for the JAR plug-in that's maven-jar-plugin.
- [plugin-in version] is the version of the plug-in you wish to download.

The best way to get these values is to know the URL where the plug-in JAR is located and to deduce these values from the URL. Figure A-1 shows an example of the URL for the JAR plug-in version 1.7 located on ibiblio. The values of artifactId, groupId, and version can easily be deduced.

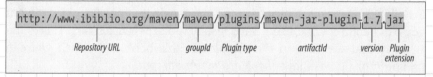

Figure A-1. Mapping between plug-in URL and groupId, artifactId, and version for the Jar plug-in v1.7

If you don't specify the Maven remote repository to use, Maven will use ibiblio by default. You can change it by defining the maven.repo.remote property (either on the command line or in your properties files). This property defines the list of remote repositories to use. For example, to specify both ibiblio and *maven-plugins.sf* you would write:

```
maven.repo.remote = http://www.ibiblio.org,http://maven-plugins.sf.net/maven
```

Note that this is probably not necessary, as the *maven-plguins.sf* repository is synced with the ibiblio one every few hours.

Please note that Chapter 2 also explains how to install a new plug-in using this strategy.

Installing a Plug-in Manually

It is also possible to install a plug-in manually. Simply download the plug-in JAR and drop it in your *MAVEN_HOME/plugins* directory (or in your *~user/.maven/plugins* directory if you wish it to be independent of your Maven installation).

Make sure to remove any previously installed version of the same plug-in, as otherwise you won't be sure which version Maven will use. If you have problems executing the new plug-in, remove the *~user/.maven/cache* Maven cache directory. It'll be re-created the next time you run Maven.

Depending on a Plug-in

It's possible to add a plug-in dependency in your project's POM. For example, to add a dependency to the JAR plug-in version 1.7, edit your project's *project.xml* and add:

```
<dependency>
  <groupId>maven</groupId>
  <artifactId>maven-jar-plugin</artifactId>
  <version>1.7</version>
</dependency>
```

If you execute a goal in this project, and if Version 1.7 of the JAR plug-in is not installed on your system, Maven will automatically download and install it. This makes it very easy to have builds that always work, even if you can't control what users have installed on their machines. This is the strategy that we used in the samples in this book and which you can find on *http://www.mavenbook.org/svn/mdn/code*.

Index

We'd like to hear your suggestions for improving our indexes. Send email to *index@oreilly.com*.

Q

QOTD application, 66
qotd:build goal, 90
quote generator, 72
QuoteGenerator, unit tests, 73

R

release announcement, 118
release tag, 112
releases, reporting, 120
remote repositories
  ibiblio repository,
      synchronization, 42
  plug-in installation, 40
remote repository
  creation, 128
  disable for offline mode, 131
  multiple, 130
  as placeholder, 130
  plug-in publishing, 179
reporting
  code best practices, 99
  duplicate code, 102
  project activity tracking, 107
  project change tracking, 111
  project content, 94
  project releases, 120
  testing status, 96
reports
  Checkstyle, 99
  custom, site genration and, 36
  Dependencies, 95
  Issue Tracking, 95
  Mailing Lists, 95
  maven-dashoard-plugin, 105
  plug-in generated, 169
  Project Team, 95
reports element, 37
repositories
  artifact sharing, 74
  remote
    creating, 128
    disable for offline mode, 131
    multiple, 130
    plug-in installation, 40
    plug-in publishing, 179
  reporting and, 94
  SCM and, 32

resources element
  copy resources, 6
  JAR plug-in and, 6
resources, plug-ins, 160
Rome, 66, 73
  Atom feeds and, 73
RSS (Really Simple Syndication)
  Rome and, 66, 73
RSync protocol, 123

S

Safari Enabled, xxiii
SCM repository, Continuous Integration
    build, 132
SCM (Source Control Management), 31
  reporting and, 94
separation-of-concerns strategy, 65
servers, proxy server configuration, 7
sharing artifacts, repository, 74
sharing, installation, 126
Simian plug-in, 103
site generation, custom reports, 36
Site plug-in, 34, 123
SNAPSHOTS, 18
SOAP services, custom goals and, 45
source control, 31
source, plug-in installation, 149
source trees, WAR plug-in, 76
SourceForge project activity
    percentage, 108
Spring Framework, dependencies
    and, 13
springframework directory, 13
StatCVS-XML plug-in, 108
static dependencies, 168
subprojects, 65
  acceptance, 81
  building all simultaneously, 86
  common configuration, 70
  contents, 66
Subversion, CruiseControl and, 133
synchronization, remote repositories
    and ibiblio repository, 42

T

tag libraries, Jelly tags, 39
tags
  contributors, 95
  dependencies, 95

About the Authors

In addition to being an active member of the Maven development team, **Vincent Massol** is the creator of the Jakarta Cactus framework. After having spent four years as a technical architect on several major projects, Vincent is now the cofounder and CTO of Pivolis, a company specializing in applying agile methodologies to offshore software development. He lives in the City of Light, Paris, France.

Timothy O'Brien is an independent consultant who lives and works in Evanston, IL, just outside Chicago. Tim is currently focused on helping clients adopt and evaluate open source software. He prefers Emacs to vi. Tim discovered programming on a TRS-80, and went on to study (and subsequently forget) electrical engineering at UVA. In his free time, Tim likes to sleep, study music, build toys with microcontrollers, and participate in open source projects. Tim contributes to the documentation and implementation of various projects at the ASF.

Colophon

Our look is the result of reader comments, our own experimentation, and feedback from distribution channels. Distinctive covers complement our distinctive approach to technical topics, breathing personality and life into potentially dry subjects.

The *Developer's Notebook* series is modeled on the tradition of laboratory notebooks. Laboratory notebooks are an invaluable tool for researchers and their successors.

The purpose of a laboratory notebook is to facilitate the recording of data and conclusions as the work is being conducted, creating a faithful and immediate history. The notebook begins with a title page that includes the owner's name and the subject of research. The pages of the notebook should be numbered and prefaced with a table of contents. Entries must be clear, easy to read, and accurately dated; they should use simple, direct language to indicate the name of the experiment and the steps taken. Calculations are written out carefully and relevant thoughts and ideas recorded. Each experiment is introduced and summarized as it is added to the notebook. The goal is to produce comprehensive, clearly organized notes that can be used as a reference. Careful documentation creates a valuable record and provides a practical guide for future developers.

Colleen Gorman was the production editor and proofreader, and Audrey Doyle was the copyeditor for *Maven: A Developer's Notebook*. Adam Witwer and Mary Anne Weeks Mayo provided quality control. Johnna VanHoose Dinse wrote the index.

Emma Colby designed the cover of this book, based on a series design by Edie Freedman. Karen Montgomery produced the cover layout with Adobe InDesign CS using the Officina Sans and JuniorHandwriting fonts.

Edie Freedman and David Futato designed the interior layout. This book was converted by Joe Wizda to FrameMaker 5.5.6 with a format conversion tool created by Erik Ray, Jason McIntosh, Neil Walls, and Mike Sierra that uses Perl and XML technologies. The text font is Adobe Boton; the heading font is ITC Officina Sans; the code font is LucasFont's TheSans Mono Condensed, and the handwriting font is a modified version of JuniorHandwriting made by Tepid Monkey Foundry, and modified by O'Reilly. The illustrations that appear in the book were produced by Robert Romano, Jessamyn Read, and Lesley Borash using Macromedia FreeHand MX and Adobe Photoshop CS. This colophon was written by Colleen Gorman.

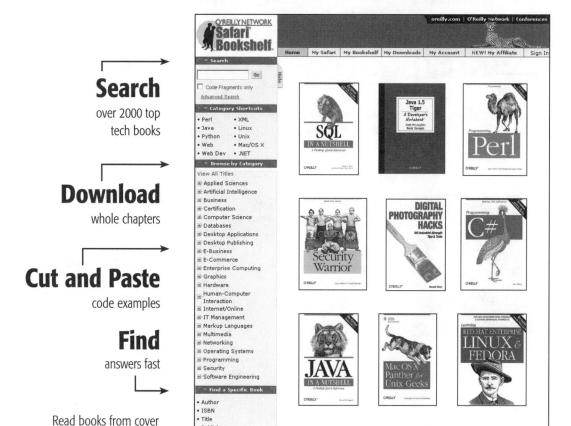

Related Titles Available from O'Reilly

Java

Ant: The Definitive Guide

Better, Faster, Lighter Java

Eclipse

Eclipse Cookbook

Enterprise JavaBeans,
4th Edition

Hardcore Java

Head First Java •

Head First Servlets & JSP

Head First EJB

Hibernate:
A Developer's Notebook

J2EE Design Patterns

Java 1.5 Tiger:
A Developer's Notebook

Java & XML Data Binding

Java & XML

Java Cookbook, *2nd Edition*

Java Data Objects

Java Database Best Practices

Java Enterprise Best Practices

Java Enterprise in a Nutshell,
2nd Edition

Java Examples in a Nutshell,
3rd Edition

Java Extreme Programming
Cookbook

Java in a Nutshell, *4th Edition*

Java Management Extensions

Java Message Service

Java Network Programming,
2nd Edition

Java NIO

Java Performance Tuning,
2nd Edition

Java RMI

Java Security, *2nd Edition*

JavaServer Faces

Java ServerPages, *2nd Edition*

Java Servlet & JSP Cookbook

Java Servlet Programming,
2nd Edition

Java Swing, *2nd Edition*

Java Web Services in a Nutshell

Learning Java, *2nd Edition*

Mac OS X for Java Geeks

Programming Jakarta Struts
2nd Edition

Tomcat: The Definitive Guide

WebLogic:
The Definitive Guide

O'REILLY®
Our books are available at most retail and online bookstores.
To order direct: 1-800-998-9938 • *order@oreilly.com* • *www.oreilly.com*
Online editions of most O'Reilly titles are available by subscription at *safari.oreilly.com*